Client Satisfaction Pays

Quality Service for Practice Success

Client Satisfaction Pays

Quality Service for Practice Success

Carin A. Smith, DVM
Stephen W. Brown, PhD
Anne-Marie Nelson, BA
Sheryl J. Bronkesh, MBA
Steven D. Wood, PhD

AAHA Press 1998

AAHA Press

12575 W. Bayaud Avenue
Lakewood, Colorado 80228

Unless otherwise noted, figures are adapted from those used in *Patient
Satisfaction Pays: Quality Service for Practice Success* (Stephen Brown et al.,
Aspen Publications, 1993)

ISBN
0-941451-71-2

Contents

Part Three: Let's Get Specific: Service Improvement for Client Retention — 143

Preface

Client Satisfaction Pays is the result of a collaboration between two groups—the American Animal Hospital Association (AAHA) and The HSM Group, Ltd., an Arizona consulting firm specializing in health-care marketing and management issues. The book is the result of several years of collaboration and work. At AAHA, Publications Consultant Debby Morehead first noticed *Patient Satisfaction Pays*, a book for physicians written by four of the co-authors of this book. AAHA had the foresight to realize that this subject is vital for veterinarians everywhere. But how would they revise it for veterinarians?

After obtaining agreement from the publisher of *Patient Satisfaction Pays* to use its book as a template, AAHA Press General Manager Dana McCullah turned to Carin A. Smith, DVM, an author with years of experience writing for and about veterinarians. Her background working in various types of practice provided just what we needed for a broad look at the many ways in which veterinarians can provide client satisfaction.

This book could not have been written without help from many others. We want to thank all of the veterinarians who took the time to talk with us and relate their ideas and thoughts to give you, the reader, the benefit of their success in satisfying pet owners while maintaining profitable practices. We also thank the practice managers, technicians, and staff members who shared their knowledge and tips. And we couldn't have written about client satisfaction without consulting the countless pet owners who told us their perceptions of what is satisfying and what is not when it comes to service in veterinary medical practices.

Thanks are also extended to Dr. Marv Johnson, Director of the Veterinary Medical Group of Des Moines, IA, and to Dr. Greg Ekdale, owner of the Highland Hospital for Animals, Bloomington, IL, for use of the mission statements from their practices; and to Dr. George Norris, Director of the Animal Hospital of Worthington, OH, for use of his client survey form. Finally, appreciation is extended to AAHA Press Advisory Board: Dr. Laurel Collins, ABVP; Dr. Richard Goebel; Dr. Charles Hickey; Dr. Clayton McKinnon; Dr. Richard Nelson, ABVP; and Dr. Hal Taylor.

The cooperative effort between AAHA and The HSM Group is an outstanding example of how veterinary and human medical fields can learn from and share with one another. We hope that this is but the first of many such collaborations.

Carin A. Smith

Stephen W. Brown

Anne-Marie Nelson

Sheryl J. Bronkesh

Steven D. Wood

About the Authors

Carin A. Smith, DVM, is a consultant and nationally recognized, award-winning author of materials for veterinarians and veterinary-related companies. Among her previous books are *Career Choices for Veterinarians: Beyond Private Practice; The Housecall Veterinarian's Manual; The Employer's Guide to Hiring Relief and Part-time Veterinarians;* and *The Relief Veterinarian's Manual* (all published by Smith Veterinary Services). She is a contributing author to Ross Clark's *Mastering the Marketplace: Taking Your Practice to the Top* (Veterinary Medicine Publishing Group).

Dr. Smith has contributed countless articles to a wide variety of veterinary publications, including the *Journal of the American Veterinary Medical Association, Veterinary Economics,* and *DVM Newsmagazine.* She works with corporate clients and multimedia companies, acting as author and editor of a variety of educational and technical materials. She also writes articles and books for pet owners, including *101 Training Tips For Your Cat* (Dell Publishing). Dr. Smith received the DVM degree from the Oregon State University – Washington State University cooperative program in 1984. Her practice experience includes work in equine, mixed, small-animal, and emergency practice.

The other authors are associated with The HSM Group, Ltd., a Scottsdale, Arizona, consulting firm specializing in health-care marketing and management issues. All are co-authors of *Patient Satisfaction Pays: Quality Service for Practice Success* (Aspen Publication, 1993); *Promoting*

Your Medical Practice: Marketing Communications for Physicians (Medical Economics Books, 1989), and *Improving Patient Satisfaction Now: How to Earn Patient and Payer Loyalty* (Aspen Publication, 1997).

Stephen W. Brown, PhD, is an internationally recognized authority on services marketing and a past president of the 50,000-member American Marketing Association. A prolific author, he has written more than a hundred articles in professional journals and 11 books. He is co-author of *Marketing Strategies for Physicians: A Guide to Practice Growth*, a reference text that was among the first on the topic of physician marketing. He is a lead editor of the first multinational book on service quality, *Service Quality: Multidisciplinary and Multinational Perspectives*, and co-edits the annual series *Advances in Services Marketing and Management*. He is professor of marketing and executive director of the Center for Services Marketing and Management at Arizona State University, as well as senior advisor to The HSM Group. In 1988 he was awarded the Academy for Health Services Marketing's coveted Philip Kotler Award. Dr. Brown obtained the doctoral degree in marketing from Arizona State University.

Anne-Marie Nelson formerly with The HSM Group is now president of Nelson and Company. During more than 20 years in the fields of public relations, marketing, and internal communications, she has held positions as hospital public relations director, marketing director for the Arizona operations of a national long-term care chain, and communications director for a dental group. A frequently published writer and an accredited business communicator, she holds the bachelor of arts degree in journalism from Northern Arizona University in Flagstaff.

Steven D. Wood, PhD, has been an active researcher, educator, and consultant in services marketing industries for more than 20 years. He has published in excess of 70 papers in professional journals and texts and given over 150 presentations to various organizations. Dr. Wood obtained his master's degree in business, with mathematics minors, from San Diego State University, and the doctoral degree from the University of Wisconsin-

Madison in quantitative business analysis, with minors in strategy and computer science. In addition to being vice chairman of The HSM Group, he is a professor of marketing in the College of Business at Arizona State University.

Sheryl J. Bronkesh, MBA, is president of The HSM Group. She has headed public relations and marketing departments for a 700-bed teaching hospital, a community hospital, and a major multihospital system. She has authored numerous professional articles and is a frequent speaker at national conferences and seminars. Ms. Bronkesh has won several national and regional awards for her work and is active in a number of health-care marketing associations on national and local levels. She was graduated magna cum laude with the bachelor of arts degree in communications from American University and earned a master of business administration degree from Arizona State University.

For information about HSM, contact: The HSM Group, Ltd., 4725 North Scottsdale Road, Suite 351, Scottsdale, Arizona 85251; 602-947-8078.

For information about Smith Veterinary Services, contact: Smith Veterinary Services, PO Box 254, Leavenworth WA 98826; 509-763-2052.

For information about the American Animal Hospital Association, contact: AAHA, PO Box 150899, Denver CO 80215-0899; 303-986-2800.

Introduction

We wrote this book for everyone who wants to provide the best possible patient care and client service. We know you understand and practice quality medicine, but you could use help and ideas for improving quality of service and client satisfaction. We believe—and numerous veterinarians have confirmed—that client satisfaction does pay. It solidifies loyalty and compliance, attracts new clients, and can improve productivity and efficiency in veterinary practice.

We've seen enough veterinarians and practices to know that some stay in control, maintain professional satisfaction, and keep growing numbers of clients happy even while wave after wave of change and upheaval wash over the veterinary profession. We believe that something can be learned from practices with a powerful commitment to client satisfaction—their attitudes, methods, and results.

We interviewed veterinarians across the United States, in solo and group practices, in rural and urban areas; house-call veterinarians; veterinarians with one clinic and those who managed more than one; and veterinary specialists. Some were AAHA-certified practices, and others were not. We questioned these veterinarians about their attitudes and beliefs as well as their activities and interactions. We queried everyone about communication, client expectations, and the role of their staff, and we spoke to their staff members and their clients. We reviewed client comments gathered as part of the *AAHA 1995 Report* to let you know what matters to pet owners. We reviewed the "Featured Practices" in

AAHA's *Trends* magazine, looking for gems and tips that were well worth passing on.

As we visited with veterinarians and reviewed their practices, we noticed—as you will—that although they have similarities, every practice has a unique style and a different approach to client care and satisfaction. For example, we visited a house-call veterinarian who takes and returns every telephone call herself, and with a veterinary ophthalmologist who had a client tell her he wished that she could be his own physician, because of the quality of care his pet received.

The veterinarians and employees we interviewed aren't perfect. Like everyone, they make mistakes, work longer hours than they might like, and deal with the entanglements of collecting bills and juggling paperwork. But they have a vision, a goal that keeps them going and keeps them committed. This book is designed to guide you and your staff in improving service quality so that you, like them, will achieve client satisfaction in *your* practice.

As you'll learn, client satisfaction is whatever your clients say it is. No matter how many articles or studies you read about what the "average" client wants, you won't know what *your* clients want until you ask them. We'll take you for a walk in your clients' shoes and then show you how to find out what they want.

Because client satisfaction depends on efforts from the entire veterinary team, we've devoted a good portion of our book to how you deal with your staff—starting with effective leadership. We'll show you that when your staff members are stimulated by challenge at work, are happy with their working conditions, and are treated well by others, your clients will benefit. You'll find that if you treat your staff as if their needs come first, they'll do the same for your clients. An added benefit, reduced staff turnover, will save you time and money.

Speaking of staff members, we know that the manager of your practice often takes on much of the work behind client satisfaction. We've devoted one chapter to practice managers only. In reality, that person may be the one who reads this book most thoroughly and leads the practice in applying its concepts.

Once you have mapped out your approach and your team is behind you, it's time to get specific with improvement in your service. We give special attention to two areas that need work in every practice: the telephone and the daily appointment schedule. You'll learn how to create a consistently friendly and efficient phone-answering procedure and how to design a schedule that fits your needs and the clients'.

Getting clients past the phone and into the exam room is only the first step. We'll show you why effective communication is essential in keeping clients satisfied. Building rapport makes pet owners feel like they are partners with you in their pets' health care and ties them to your practice. We'll show you how. Finally, we'll address a myriad of other service improvement tips and client retention strategies that will satisfy your clients *and* improve your bottom line.

We know that good ideas often don't go any farther than the discussion stage unless you follow concrete steps. Thus, each chapter concludes with a series of Action Steps, a summary for you to take with you and apply to your everyday work.

You'll find that if you devote the time and effort to satisfying your clients, you'll be more satisfied, too. Enjoy your pursuit!

Part One

Your Client Comes First

Client satisfaction pays. We'll explain why and how that's true and give you a starting point for taking a new approach to your practice. You can find out what your clients want and need by stepping into their shoes. If you walk through your practice like a client, you may be surprised at what you learn.

Your next step is to find out what your clients want. If you make assumptions, they may be wrong. We'll show you a variety of techniques to evaluate client expectations.

One thing all clients expect is that you inform them about their pets' health care. Medical information can be confusing and complicated. Giving your clients the information they need—in a way they understand—is vital to client satisfaction. We'll show you how.

Chapter 1

Client Satisfaction Does Pay

Q. What is client satisfaction?
A. Whatever the client says it is.

Opinions and definitions of quality service and client satisfaction are as numerous as zip codes. In our opinion, though, *client satisfaction is what each client says it is*. It is determined by each individual according to his or her needs and experiences. It also is determined by the actions and interactions of the people and processes that surround your practice. You can't always meet a client's every need or expectation, but if you show personal concern, your clients usually will be satisfied nevertheless.

Chances are that you went into veterinary medicine because you care about animals and believe you can make a difference using your veterinary education, training, and expertise. You're dedicated to excellence in veterinary care, and you know what *you* believe quality service to be.

Many of us have a similar, simple philosophy: "I try to treat every one of my clients as I would my best friend, and each patient as I would my own animal." You believe this approach helps personalize the care you and your staff provide. As a veterinarian, you go home at the end of the day, look in the mirror, and feel good about what you've done.

You are a concerned, competent professional who strives to achieve the best possible outcome for every client. Like many other veterinarians, though, you sometimes feel overwhelmed with the financial obstacles, encroaching demands from government regulations, and pressures from competing practices that seem to get in the way of quality care. You're trying to make a personal connection, and at the same time you're wondering how you're going to explain that your fees are going up. You've seen other veterinarians frantically focus on administrative and cost issues, sometimes at the expense of client satisfaction, and you swear that won't happen to you. But it's the nonveterinary stuff that wears you down!

Service: A Business Strategy

Patients don't care how much you know until they know how much you care.—Sir William Osler

Pet owners are concerned not only about the medical care their pets receive but also about the service they themselves receive: how their veterinarian communicates with them, how the practice staff treats them and their pets, and the kind of information they are given. In recent years the veterinary community has discovered that clients expect quality service, and it also makes sound business sense. Most veterinarians today are closely scrutinizing their attitudes, activities, and processes and taking steps to improve them. Creating a patient- and client-first focus enhances the personal relationship at the heart of quality veterinary care.

The effort is worth it. Client satisfaction is a dollars-and-*sense* issue. It's an economic success factor. Veterinarians we interviewed know their clients evaluate not only cost but also proof of value. Practices that pay special attention to when, where, and especially *how* service is provided see results on the bottom line in lower costs and greater profitability, and at the top in increased revenues.

Savvy veterinarians are asking their clients their opinions and are using what they learn to improve the

Client Satisfaction Pays

Here's how:

+ Greater profitability
+ Improved client retention
+ Increased client referrals
+ Improved compliance
+ Reduced risk of malpractice suits
+ Personal and professional fulfillment

+ Improved productivity
+ Better staff morale
+ Reduced staff turnover
+ Improved collections
+ Greater efficiency

quality of their service, to anticipate and exceed client expectations. They are reaping the rewards of putting the client at the top of their organization: client loyalty, staff loyalty and motivation, improved productivity, better compliance, lower risk for malpractice suits. Whether you call it client satisfaction or customer service, it does pay.

As evidence that quality service pays off:

+ It costs five to six times more to acquire a new client than it does to do business with a current client.[1]

+ Happy clients will tell three to five people about their positive experience. Dissatisfied clients will tell up to 20 people about their problem.[2]

+ A major source of client frustration, and one that often leads to lawsuits, is the veterinarian's failure to communicate.[3]

Mining Diamonds: Investing in Client Satisfaction

Quality service means a lot of things to a lot of people. You may interpret it differently than your partner or the veterinarian next door. As long as quality *veterinary care* is at the heart of it, there are a variety of acceptable ways to provide good service. The four key elements of quality service are:

1. *Customer.* The customer is the reason for all your efforts.

2. *Commitment.* Without commitment you will achieve nothing that is meaningful.

3. *Expectations.* You must know your client's expectations to satisfy, manage, or exceed them.

Figure 1.1 The Quality Diamond

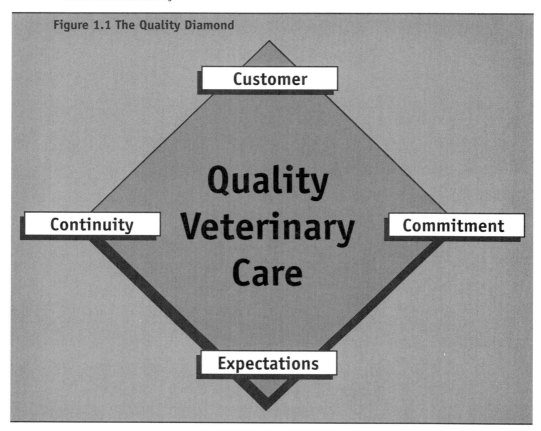

4. *Continuity.* Like a cat with diabetes dependent on insulin, service demands continuity through daily attention and continual improvement.

These four facets of quality service constitute what we call the Quality Diamond, because a focus on quality is like mining diamonds (see Figure 1.1). The gems you bring forth are client satisfaction, staff motivation, professional fulfillment, and practice success.

Most veterinarians understand quality in general, and quality veterinary care in particular, but you're not always clear on the finer points of quality service: how, where, when, who, and even sometimes what and why? That's where the framework of the Quality Diamond comes in. It's based on the belief that quality must be inherent in every thought, attitude, action, and process, with the needs of the client—your customer— foremost.

Customer

You may be surprised at our use of the term *customer* for your clients. But if the client, the pet owner who comes to you for help, isn't your customer, who is? Your clients use your services. The service you provide happens to be veterinary care, which makes it somewhat more personal than, say, getting a haircut or buying a car. The personal aspect of veterinary care makes satisfying your clients— knowing what your customers' wants and needs are— even more critical for the health of your practice.

The idea of client as customer puts things in a whole new light, doesn't it? Customers can be demanding, annoying, unrealistic, loud, and objectionable. Or they can be pleasant, easygoing, intelligent, accommodating, and knowledgeable. They also can be timid, questioning, unprepared, lacking knowledge, and uncertain about what they want or need. (Hmmm… Sounds very much like *your* clients, doesn't it?) Because businesses depend on them to stay in business, customers are given the benefit of the doubt. They get good service no matter who they are or how they act (within reasonable limits).

We use the term *customer* in referring to your clients to emphasize and encourage a frame of reference—an attitude that may be somewhat different from what you may have learned in veterinary school or in practice. Clients traditionally were deferential; customers can be demanding. What's more, the client persona is changing. You've probably noticed that many of your clients are no longer passive, unquestioning recipients of your veterinary benevolence. This is especially true of the baby boomers, who tend to be less familiar with and less tolerant of the patriarchal, autocratic-style veterinarian. More educated and more demanding, these clients have a liberated, interactive view of their role. They see themselves as participants with a voice in the veterinary encounter.

By viewing clients as customers, veterinarians acknowledge client equality and rights in the veterinarian-client relationship. Viewing clients as customers encourages an effort to understand and meet their needs. Your customers want to participate actively in decisions about their pets, including the selection of veterinarians and even, to some extent, the treatment that may be required. They believe that they have rights and that veterinarians have responsibilities. They seek value for their veterinary dollar, especially because their pets aren't insured for veterinary care and the owner must pay directly for it. Discriminating, quality-conscious customers say that better quality care has greater value.

Consider this[4]:

✦ In choosing a veterinarian, 45% of pet owners cited *recommendation* as the most important factor. The second most frequent response (27%) was location.

✦ Only 3% cited *price* as the most important factor, and only 7% listed price as *any* factor in their choice of a veterinarian.

In our discussion of the customer, we use the singular reference: the *customer*. We do this because we want to reinforce the idea that each client should be viewed as an individual, not an anonymous member of a demographic, psychographic, or other group with aggregate needs, concerns, and experiences. *Each client is unique, with specific personalized needs and expectations.*

When you begin to categorize, compartmentalize, or pigeonhole your clients, you depersonalize them. Your patient becomes "the cat abscess in exam room 2," and the client is "the nervous old lady on the phone." In turn, you may begin to tune out individual needs and concerns in the mistaken belief that you know what all owners of pets with that condition or ailment want or need. Even though you may have treated thousands of flea-infested dogs, each of their owners is singular and unique.

In businesses and practices with a service orientation, the customer is at the top of the organization chart, just as we've placed the customer at the top of the Quality Diamond in the figure. It's where your customer belongs in the organization chart for your practice.

Commitment

If you're *interested* in something, you do it when you have time.

If you're *committed* to something, you make time to do it.

Commitment begins with the veterinarian. This holds true whether you're a solo practitioner (and thus the acting head of the practice) or the newest veterinarian in a group of 10. Commitment means making an emotional and intellectual pledge to a *course of action*. If you truly believe that clients have rights that extend beyond accurate diagnosis and treatment, you can't help but be committed. If you're committed to your clients and to quality in practice, you'll embrace quality improvement as a necessary ongoing behavior and attitude in your practice, and you'll convey this attitude to your staff.

Whether you are the head of the practice or one of many veterinarians in a group, your commitment to quality service must be 100%—as much a part of the care you provide as your skilled surgical technique, a well-researched diagnosis, and treatment that's clinically effective and appropriate for your patients. If you are half-hearted or hesitant about the importance of service excellence, you are not truly committed. Employees and practice colleagues will know that you don't mean what you say and they are likely to reflect *your* attitude in *their* behavior toward each other and with clients.

By the way, when we speak of you or your practice, we're referring to every kind of practice: solo, partnership, or corporate; rural or urban; small animal, large animal, or specialty practice. And when we speak to *you*, we mean *every veterinarian* in the practice. (We mention this because some veterinarians in group practices say, "I'm not the leader—that's Dr. Jones, the practice owner." These individuals may not view themselves as *the* leader of their practice, *but their clients and staff do*.) We also include the office or practice manager, as well as other supervisors or team leaders, because in many practices those people are the second tier of influence. Employees view the person in this position as the veterinarian's surrogate when management issues are concerned.

The examples set and the decisions made by you, your partners or associates, and your practice manager, are observed carefully. Like it or not, your example and decisions are what your team members will heed, believe, and emulate. We mention this as both disclaimer and encouragement. To achieve results, you need to understand your influence and power and use it ethically and effectively.

Commitment to client satisfaction may be shown in many ways. For example, Dr. Paul Rowan shows his commitment through community education. As the hospital director at Owl Creek Veterinary Hospital in Virginia Beach, VA, Dr. Rowan provided an Animal Rescue Class that taught pet owners about common poisons, first aid, and CPR. His staff offered a similar program in the local school system to teach kids how to handle and care for family pets. Students viewed radiographs, learned how to pick up a real puppy or kitten correctly, and listened to a pet's heart with a stethoscope. Each student was given a "pet care expert" certificate and a coupon to be applied to a hospital visit.[5]

Clocktower Animal Hospital in Herndon, VA, was built with client concerns in mind. Windows abound, and two walls of the surgery room are glass. Clients can view much of the hospital's activity, including the procedures being performed on their own pets.[6]

At Westside Veterinary Hospital in New York City, one sign of commitment to client satisfaction is the computerized scheduling system. It allows any doctor, technician, or receptionist anywhere in the building to access the schedule and make an appointment. Thus, a doctor making a follow-up phone call can schedule a pet's recheck exam without transferring that client to a receptionist.[7]

Expectations

A housecall veterinarian clearly recalls a story told to her in veterinary school more than 10 years ago:

> *While we were on clinical rotation, our instructor told us about a client who brought her pet to the clinic intending to have its teeth cleaned. She said something like, "My dog is here to be put to sleep and have its teeth cleaned." Apparently the second part of the statement was not heard. When she came that afternoon to pick up her dog, she discovered that it had been "put to sleep." This story has stuck*

with me all these years, because of the strong impression it made about the need for clear communication.

Miscommunication leads to false expectations. It often involves management of diseases that cannot be cured. Many of us recall times we've seen an animal with a chronic ear or skin problem. We may briefly discuss the ongoing nature of the problem, but the pet owner understands only that he's been given some cream to apply to the troubled area. When he returns for the third follow-up visit, he seems irritated that we haven't "cured" the problem.

What we have here is a failure to communicate, an inability by clients to voice their needs and a lack of understanding of client expectations by veterinarians. Miscommunication like this demonstrates the need for understanding client expectations about the veterinary process and all of the related activities and evidence that surround it. If you don't take the time and effort to discern what your clients anticipate from their veterinary encounter, and what their needs and concerns are, you may make the mistake of assuming that you know what they want or what they hope to gain.

In contrast, with accurate knowledge of client expectations, veterinarian and staff time and effort are invested in doing things superbly rather than constantly fixing things that went wrong. This is more productive and satisfying for everyone. Certainly, your experience can speed the diagnostic process. It lets you know immediately what a set of symptoms may point to, allowing you to eliminate certain possibilities, and it also acts as a filter. You see only what your experience tells you to expect. Experience, especially after countless clients and years of practice, can block change and new beliefs or attitudes.

Many veterinarians have told us, "I *know* what my clients want and what they need." When we survey their clients to learn how satisfied these clients are and what they expect, though, the responses surprise these veterinarians. For example, when pet owners were queried about the services their own veterinarians offered, 34% did not know whether dental services were available, and 51% were unsure whether their veterinarians offered access to a specialist. Yet, 81% knew whether their veterinarian sold pet food.[8]

As *Service America* authors Albrecht and Zemke point out, *the longer you've been in business, the more likely it is that you really don't know what your customer wants.*[9] Setting aside assumptions and putting a ruler to reality allows you to develop measurable service parameter standards that yield more predictable and consistent service outcomes. In the chapters to come, you'll learn about ways to measure and evaluate client expectations.

Continuity

Continuity means continuous, consistent, ever improving, and never ending. It encompasses all the ways and means for measuring, evaluating, and monitoring your progress. With continuity, quality is a built-in attribute of every activity. It becomes a habit. And habits, as we all know, are hard to break. To highlight its qualities:

✦ Continuity is service that gets better day after day. It is continuous improvement in practice. Continuity formalizes the act of examining every practice activity and asks, "Is there a better way? Can we do this with more care, faster, slower, or more thoroughly? Are we doing everything possible to keep our clients comfortable, educated, and informed? Should we speed up? Slow down? Eliminate steps? Add steps? Can someone else do this better?"

✦ Continuity means understanding that what you do today may not be appropriate or effective tomorrow. Things change. People change. Continuity requires continuous measurement: asking questions, seeking answers, updating your beliefs, and changing your behaviors. It means doing every little thing a little bit better every day and looking for little things as well as big things to improve. It means making *status quo* a couple of dirty words and praising mistakes if they result from trying new ideas. It also means making amends when mistakes happen and seeking ways to avoid them in the future.

✦ Continuity means looking beyond veterinary medicine at what other industries are doing to ensure excellent service and customer satisfaction. This concept, called *benchmarking*, brings innovation into the practice. It leads to paradigm shifts—stepping out of the veterinarian box that contains all the activities and beliefs that surround what is typical or expected in a veterinary practice. Benchmarking helps you open the windows of your mind, letting in the breeze of new ideas.

✦ Continuity begins by setting standards for service. We call them *minimum requirements for maximum performance*. Like practice parameters for clinical care, service standards are specific requirements that ensure consistency.

Continuous improvement requires commitment and participation from everyone in the practice. In the following chapters you'll learn how other practices encourage enthusiastic participation and knowledgeable decisions from their staffs. You can't do it by yourself. Effective change calls for effective, motivated people.

No Shortcuts to Quality

The Quality Diamond describes what we believe are the four critical elements of quality service. In addition, we offer these caveats:

✦ Don't ignore or minimize the importance of any of the elements of the Quality Diamond. Each is critical.

✦ Accept that, in creating client satisfaction, *how* care is delivered is as important as the clinical care itself.

✦ Include *all* of your staff members. Your staff is so important that we've devoted a lot of space in this book exclusively to their role.

✦ Be willing to give new ideas and new methods time to work.

To make quality second nature and to provide quality service, you must *plan* to do so. A lack of planning, as well as the "Wednesday is Quality Day" mentality, is what defeats efforts to provide quality service.

Figure 1.2 Whose Needs Come First in Your Practice?

If Practice Needs Come First		*If Patient Needs Come First*
A practice that puts clients after the needs of the doctors and staff may respond in the following way:		A practice that views clients as customers takes this approach:

| Client calls are seen as interruptions and client visits as disruptions that must be tolerated. | **Service Orientation**  | "How can we serve you?" is the guiding principle for how doctors and staff deal with each other, referral sources, and clients. |

| Telephone calls are put on hold, answered and returned as it meets the needs of the practice and staff. | **Telephone** | Every telephone call is viewed as a person with a need to be met, not just a voice. |

| Schedule is set up according to the convenience of the doctor, staff, or a rigid appointment book. | **Scheduling**  | Practice hours are determined with the clients' needs in mind. Surveys are taken periodically to ensure that current hours of operation are convenient. |

| Clients are moved to the exam room just to get them out of the way, not because the doctor is ready to see them. Decor, furnishings, and layout are designed to meet the needs of doctors and staff. | **Comfort and Environment** 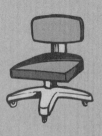 | Clients are moved to exam rooms early if their pets are uncomfortable around others in the waiting room; otherwise, they're allowed to wait where they are most comfortable. Decor and furnishings are tailored to client comfort along with the functional needs of the doctors and staff. |

The doctor focuses primarily on obtaining information quickly during the medical history taking. Little time is allotted to client questions. If a client requests additional information, the doctor may offer a pamphlet without discussing it.

Interaction

Clients are asked open-ended questions that encourage them to express concerns or questions. Printed or video information is important but secondary to face-to-face education.

Quality care is viewed as consisting only of accurate diagnosis, appropriate treatment, and the best possible outcome for the circumstances and pet's condition. Waiting time and staff attitude are considered noncritical.

Quality

Quality care is understood by doctors and staff to encompass relationship issues, comfort, waiting time, and staff attitude, as well as medical, surgical, and technical skills.

Client follow-up is considered unnecessary except for serious conditions.

Follow-up

Follow-up is critical, providing feedback and opportunity for clients to bring up forgotten or unaddressed issues.

Specialists to whom clients are referred are viewed as separate and distinct from the practice. Referrals are kept to a minimum.

Referrals

Specialists to whom clients are referred are viewed as a reflection of practice quality. Client opinion of consultants is solicited. Referrals or consultations are considered a sign of a quality practice.

Doctor is considered to be "the highest authority." Client opinion counts only peripherally.

Client Perception

The client is considered to be the "ultimate authority" in evaluating the veterinary experience.

Quality consultant Tom Vanderpool was quoted in the *Wall Street Journal* as saying that many companies don't see results and may tire of trying because they isolate quality programs from daily operations. "They tend to put it off as something special, as an objective with 10,000 activities unto itself," he says. "It is not. It's a way to meet business objectives."[10]

If you or your staff think of quality as a program or a slogan rather than a habit and an attitude, it'll doom you to defeat every time. Says Steven Walleck of McKinsey & Co., a national consulting firm, "Most [quality programs] require so much groundwork before results can be expected that you're almost systematically doomed."[11]

We believe one of the surest routes to failure is trying to turn quality service into a program. A belief in quality must be an internal attitude, not a slogan on a poster.

The Quality Diamond is designed to help you overcome the biggest barriers to service quality

✦ Misplaced practice priorities

✦ Lack of commitment

✦ Not knowing where to start

✦ Treating quality as an add-on

✦ Trying to do too much too quickly

The Quality Diamond: A Framework for Success

The Quality Diamond is a framework for understanding service quality and its important components. It gives structure to a concept—quality—that sometimes can seem as difficult to touch, feel, or describe as clouds in the sky. The Quality Diamond brings quality down to earth and makes it tangible. It starts with the customer. It needs your commitment, an understanding of expectations, and continuity, continuous improvement day by day, year in, year out. It isn't simple, but it's manageable, and it has rewards on the bottom line, in professional fulfillment, in staff satisfaction, and especially, in satisfied clients.

Just as pet owners have a choice of veterinarians, you have a choice. You can create a practice environment that encourages and rewards improvement, innovation, and personal attention to your customers (Figure 1.2). You can lead your satisfied clients to better health care for their pets, and in the process improve the health of your practice and your satisfaction with veterinary medicine. Or you can adopt an alternative thought, the belief of a few veterinarians we know who say, "I *am* quality!", who believe that quality resides in the veterinary degree. Although they are providing technical quality of care, many of these veterinarians and their practices are foundering in a veterinary environment that demands change to achieve progress, satisfaction, and success.

Change is constant in veterinary medicine, and choices are everywhere. Your customers are making choices every day that affect your bottom line. You, too, have a choice. You can choose to put your customer at the top of your organization, making customer satisfaction the guiding principle of your practice and motivating your staff to give your customers superior veterinary care and service. Or, by refusing to change, you can allow external forces to direct your future and determine your success. What's your choice?

Notes

1. R. Gerson. *Beyond Customer Service: Keeping Clients for Life*. Menlo Park, CA: Crisp Publications, 1994: 3,13.
2. Gerson.
3. J. Dinsmore, DVM. Veterinary Lawsuits: Trends and Defense Strategies. In *Veterinary Clinics of North America, Small Animal Practice: Legal Issues Affecting Veterinary Practice*, Sept 1993: 1024.
4. American Animal Hospital Association. *1995 AAHA Report: A Study of the Companion Animal Veterinary Services Market*:15.
5. A. Ashby. Grow Your Practice. *AAHA Trends*, May 1995:17–19.
6. Ashby. Clocktower Animal Hospital. *AAHA Trends*, Dec/Jan 1995:13–14.
7. Ashby. Practice Reflects a High Level of Care. *AAHA Trends*, Aug/Sep 1993:15–16.
8. AAHA *1995 Report: 100–101*.
9. K. Albrecht and R. Zemke. *Service America*. Homewood, IL: Dow Jones-Irwin, 1985.
10. G. Fuchsberg. Quality Programs Show Shoddy Results. *Wall Street Journal*, May 14, 1992: B-1.10.
11. Fuchsberg, B-9.

Chapter 2

A Walk in Your Client's Shoes

Every veterinary experience is a compilation of expectations and processes—an accumulation of moments of truth.

You're sitting in a darkened theater, enveloped in the turmoil and troubles of the characters of the action-packed film. Suddenly someone pipes up loudly, "Ha! Look at that car in the background! It's a 1949 Buick— and this movie is supposed to take place in 1943!" He continues to point out flaws until an usher shushes him. Noticing the errors diminishes your enjoyment of the film briefly, but soon you're engrossed once again, the production glitches and outrageous script forgotten.

The next day your mate talks you into going to another movie. You arrive late at the theater and discover that the only seats left are in the second row from the front, but you stay because the movie has received four-star reviews. Twenty minutes into the movie, you wonder how anyone could rave about this witless, plotless movie. The longer you sit, the more you find to dislike, from the music (too raucous) to the humor (nonexistent) to the popcorn (stale).

The rating you give each movie contrasts dramatically. One had mistakes, but you overlooked them because the overall experience was favorable. "Two thumbs up!" you rhapsodize to colleagues the next day. In the second movie every error in production, lighting, scripting, and theater ambience confirmed and compounded your opinion. "Trash!" you pronounce it.

We don't want to compare veterinary medicine to movie making—one is real life and life giving, and the other is fictional entertainment—but they have some similarities in how each experience is evaluated. Every veterinary experience is a compilation of expectations, personalities, and processes. Like the moviegoer rating a film, a client's overall evaluation of his or her experience depends on the total picture, the accumulated moments of truth, not one individual frame. People aren't perfect, and processes have many parts, so mistakes sometimes occur. From the highly trained staff and structured activities of New York's Animal Medical Center to the unpredictable pace of the one-veterinarian, one-employee practice in rural America, service slip-ups happen. Even in the most tightly organized, customer-oriented practice, employees, veterinarians, and clients get short tempered, schedules get delayed, reports get misfiled, and phone calls get put on indefinite hold.

One incident is not likely to result in complete dissatisfaction. Clients who know you and your staff and who know that your normal practice style is efficient, friendly, and customer centered will forgive the noisy reception room—once. They will overlook having their phone call transferred to three different people if it seldom happens. They may ask more insistently for details about their dog's scheduled cystotomy if they believe you haven't explained the procedure as clearly as you usually do. If a bill arrives showing a balance due that they've already paid, they will call your bookkeeper with confusion, not anger, in their voice if this is a rare occurrence.

People are amazingly forgiving of the occasional slip-up, as long as your overall service attitude emphasizes caring and quality. Here's how a client may subconsciously process her experience:

> *The doctor was friendly and informative; the staff was courteous; the clinic was clean and conveniently located. I waited only 10 minutes in the reception area. The receptionist seemed preoccupied*

during check-out, but that's the exception. The doctor gave me a videotape to look at because she figured out that I needed more information, and she told me to call if my dog's condition didn't clear up in a week. She seemed rushed, but the place was busy, and usually she gives me her full attention.

Clients also tend to evaluate each visit to your practice from the perspective of their needs at the time, which may change from week to week. A client who works as a secretary, who is docked for every moment she is gone from work, may put a high priority on being seen on time when she has taken time from her job for her bird's routine examination. Last month, when she brought her bird for a fit-in appointment because of a sudden onset of lethargy, getting full information about the condition and how to treat her bird was far more important than the dollars she lost from her paycheck because she had to wait an hour.

In this chapter we'll look in detail at the typical client visit, helping you see your practice through your clients' eyes. We'll help you eliminate the activities and processes that hinder both productivity and satisfaction, and smooth the rough edges that irritate and diminish the professionalism of your practice. By getting up close and personal, we'll help you see where a new approach, a better attitude, or a different way of doing things can make all the difference in the snapshot that clients have of your practice.

Creating First Impressions

The vet I used to go to had an extremely dirty office that always smelled bad.—California client

The vet I used to go to performed unnecessary and costly procedures on my pet.—Iowa pet owner

The doctor was ignorant of customer service. He had a used-car salesman attitude. He was shifty with his prices and cost information.—California client

I didn't believe the vet cared about my pet. It seemed like he was only doing his job.—Washington pet owner[1]

Just as Mom told you when you were growing up, you never get a second chance to make a good first impression. That first impression sets your clients' expectations for their encounter with your practice and sets the tone for your relationship.

Let's say that you and your staff are committed to taking good care of your clients and that you'd like to start off on the right foot (or feet). How do you fulfill your clients' expectations? How do you make a good impression every time? The first step is to look at your practice from your clients' perspective. To do so, you first must know who your clients are.

The *1995 AAHA Report* has described "typical" pet owner demographics: The majority (69%) are married and many (60%–64%) do not have children under 18 living at home. Ages of pet owners are evenly spaced across the spectrum. [1]

Who is *your* typical client? Are many of your clients elderly, with hearing or vision loss? Young couples with small children? Busy professionals? The idea is to walk, see, and listen from your clients' multiple perspectives. Think through every step they take in getting veterinary care in your practice.

Extending A Warm Welcome

Do you make it easy for potential new clients to find you? Welcoming new clients starts with their telephone contact with you. The phone is so important that we've devoted an entire chapter to its use. Chapter 11 offers detailed information about how you and your staff can make a positive first and continuing impression on the telephone.

Do you have a way to accommodate clients who are "shopping" for a veterinarian? One way to get them in is to offer a tour of the hospital and an introduction to your staff. Or allow time for courtesy get-acquainted interviews for potential clients.

Can Pet Owners Find You?

To be sure that potential clients are aware of your practice and can find you:

✦ Be sure your sign is readable and highly visible.

✦ Keep a high profile in your community by giving classes through the community school or 4-H, being involved in athletic activities, or participating in service organizations.

N

W ⟵ ⬥ ⟶ E

S

✦ Ensure that referring veterinarians and your veterinary society have current information about you, your skills, and your practice.

✦ If a large number of your clients are computer-savvy, create a web site that includes information about your practice.

✦ Ensure that your Yellow Pages listing tells clients about your services, practice hours, location(s), and other convenience features; if your clients include people whose vision is impaired, use type that's large enough for them to read.

✦ Create a brochure that describes your practice, or a newsletter that promotes your practice while it educates clients. (Tailor your marketing to the type of pet owners you want to attract. A southern California veterinarian notes, "The brochure we had at my former hospital was out of this world, but I think it turned some people off. It was big and expensive-looking. What works for one place may not work for another.")

What's your method for scheduling clients? Do you leave plenty of room in your schedule for unexpected problems? If your clients with sick pets can't get in to see you promptly, take a look at your scheduling system (you'll get help with this in Chapter 12).

When a new client is scheduled and you have time to send information by mail preceding the appointment, send a personalized letter confirming the appointment, welcoming the client to your practice, and explaining your policies and procedures. This friendly letter can set the right tone for you and your clients to work effectively together. Take care so that it doesn't come across like some letters we've seen, as a briefing on "rules of conduct for our clients." Consider enclosing a veterinary history form for the client to fill out before he or she arrives for the first appointment, and enclose a business card. It's also a nice gesture to enclose a map showing clients how to locate your practice and, in busy areas, where to park.

At Mission Animal and Bird Hospital in Oceanside, CA, Dr. Robert Cartin has an arrangement with nearby pet centers that benefits him, the pet center, and the client:

> *I examine the puppies before they are put up for sale. Then the buyers get a free initial visit. If the puppy has any problems within 60 days, they get an 80% discount, so they pay only 20%. I consider this advertising and marketing cost. If we can get them in the first time, they'll come back. I firmly believe we have to have alliances with humane societies and pet stores because they become the gatekeepers who send new pet owners to your practice.*

Dr. George Norris offers a free "Pre-Ownership Counseling Program" for prospective pet owners at the Animal Hospital of Worthington, OH. The program helps people determine what kind of pet best suits their environment and would meet their expectations. That service, along with other services the hospital offers, is listed in the hospital's brochure. To spread the word about the program, Dr. Norris also puts news releases in the newspaper, and gives talks to service organizations and at the local library.

Discussing Your Fees

When a new client calls, it's important to find out how the client intends to pay for services so that potential misunderstandings can be headed off early. Doing this without sounding offensive requires more than a little tact. One way to handle this important issue so the staff person doesn't come across sounding as if money is the first priority of the practice is to say something like this: "So you can prepare for your visit, you should know that our clinic accepts checks, MasterCard, or VISA cards for payment."

Do you make your fees known in advance to your clients? Clients appreciate knowing approximate fees before services are rendered. Although we don't necessarily recommend posting a "menu of services and prices" in your reception area, it is a good idea to have a policy, protocol, and designated staff person(s) who can discuss fees, payment options, and especially alternatives for clients with low incomes. Providing a written estimate for *all* clients whose pets are to be hospitalized (not just those who request one) reduces misunderstandings. (We'll address how to handle concerns about fees in more detail in Chapter 14.)

Providing Easy Access and Comfort

What is your parking lot like? Is the area well-lit? Is the location of your practice convenient for clients? Do they feel safe arriving and leaving? How does your landscaping look? Is the grass green and healthy and the bushes neatly trimmed? Do your windows sparkle? Can clients easily see directional signs and the entrance? Oscar London, MD, says:

A doctor's office should be decorated tastefully—but not expensively, unless he prefers a burglar over a janitor to clean up after hours.[2]

What kind of impression does your reception area leave? Do you pay more attention to your prices than to cleanliness? Is clean-up something that your staff "gets around to?" Would you be better off to hire a regular janitorial service? The *1995 AAHA Report* found that *more people switched veterinarians because of a dirty facility than because of prices.*[3] Your entire practice, including the entryway, should be immaculate. Although wiping fingerprints off the glass doors and keeping floors swept or vacuumed can be time-consuming in a busy practice, a dirty or messy appearance sends a message you don't want your clients to hear.

"When we arrive here in the morning, we look at how many fingerprints have been left on the glass in front of the hospital," says Dr. Bill Swartz, hospital director of Clocktower Animal Hospital in Herndon, VA.[4] That attention to detail is applied to every aspect of his practice.

We all can't afford the latest decor, but your paint should be clean and not peeling. (A fresh coat of paint is not that expensive and is fairly easy to apply.) If your carpet or vinyl flooring shows distinctive wear patterns, it's time to replace it. The colors and patterns chosen should be ones that don't become dated. We all can spot the 70's shag carpet, and certain colors and styles from the 90's will be just as distinctively dated.

Does your waiting area offer cat owners a peaceful place to wait apart from rambunctious dogs? Do you have a "holding pen" for pets whose owners have their hands full with children or paperwork? Extra leashes for those who forget their own?

Does your selection of magazines reflect diverse client interests? It probably includes magazines such as the *AKC Gazette* and *Cat Fancy*, but what about *Organic Gardening, Wired, Food & Wine, Working Mother,* and *Highlights for Children*? Why not ask your clients what they would like to read?

Your reception area can be a place to educate your clients. A rack with brochures and helpful articles is a good idea. You can supplement this with information about community services and agencies, special events, and pet behavior or training classes. Local agencies and organizations will be happy to keep you stocked with information and updates. Some practices provide VCRs with tapes about common disorders, educational posters, or bulletin boards with notices of interest to clients. Others use displays (call it a "museum!") of a dog skeleton, kidney stones, or intestinal parasites in jars (kids love these). This sends a message that you're just as interested in helping pets stay healthy as you are in treating their illnesses.

Gynecologists and other medical specialists whose clients are predominantly women recognize that comfort is a significant first-impression factor. Veterinarians should take heed—about 87% of your clients are women.[5]

What do you do about clients who want to visit their hospitalized pets? Clients appreciate the special attention they receive at Westside Veterinary Hospital in New York City. The "visiting room" allows clients to spend time with hospitalized pets in a comfortable atmosphere.[6]

Waiting Room Comfort and Convenience

Does your waiting area provide these amenities?

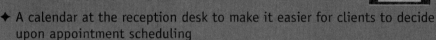

◆ Comfortable seating that is easy to get into and out of by older people, pregnant women, and clients with arthritis or orthopedic problems

◆ Windows and plants

◆ Drinking water and tissues

◆ Light refreshments (choose food and drinks that are healthy and easy to keep tidy, and place them out of reach of wagging tails)

◆ A calendar at the reception desk to make it easier for clients to decide upon appointment scheduling

◆ A phone in a private area for clients who must call family members to discuss and decide upon treatment options or euthanasia

◆ If many of your clients have small children, child-sized chairs and a table

◆ A room configuration that allows private conversations that are not easily overheard. Receptionists should be trained to speak in low tones and to adjourn to a private room when discussions with clients touch on personal or sensitive issues

◆ A well-marked and easily accessible restroom with an easily located light switch (Who is in charge of cleaning the restroom and making sure the toilet paper roll isn't empty?)

Take a seat in your exam room and stay there for 15 minutes. Does it have seating for two or three people? Are the rooms well ventilated, or do they get stuffy and hot when several people are there? Is reading material available? Something to entertain children?

The exam room should reflect your professionalism. In some hospitals, technicians place a placard on each exam table after it has been cleaned in between appointments, stating: "This table has been cleaned and disinfected."

Walking Through the Appointment

One technique for understanding client needs is to ask a friend or staff member to play the role of a client and to walk him or her through a typical client appointment. Role-playing helps the staff identify bottlenecks and less-than-excellent service encounters at each point or moment of truth in the practice. From the initial telephone call for an appointment through diagnostic testing, exam room interactions, check-out, and billing, "Joe Client" prods for problems: "Okay, I've checked in at the front desk and you've told me to have a seat. What happens to me now? And what's happening in the front and back to get ready for me?" This step-by-step process forces staff and veterinarians to see and hear actions and responses through the client's eyes and ears and thus helps them determine where improvements should be made and standards set.

Most employees are acutely aware of the glitches and goof-ups that are likely to occur as clients make their way through the maze of people and processes in the practice. Often, however, this is an eye-opening exercise for veterinarians. You become aware of barriers, hoops, and hurdles that clients confront in your practice—barriers that often are shielded from your view.

Showing You Care

You will win your clients' hearts by showing you care about them and their pets. This can be demonstrated by celebrating pets' birthdays, acknowledging clients' children, and sharing your personal interests.

Special techniques can make procedures easier on pets—and thus on their owners. For instance, one veterinarian had a client whose fractious diabetic cat required sedation just to take a blood sample for routine blood glucose screening. The client was ready to give up on the case when the doctor learned that she could obtain a sufficient blood sample from the cat simply by pricking an ear vein. The cat did not need to be re-strained and didn't object, so the routine blood test became routine indeed.

Another veterinarian uses a "slide across the table" technique for administering injections to cats. She performs the injection with one hand while holding the cat by its scruff and sliding it gently across the exam table with the other hand. The result is that further restraint isn't needed, the cat does not object, and the owners are amused.

Caring for Your "Internal Customers"

Your staff members are your internal customers. *People treat others as they are treated.* The CEO of a highly successful company, William Marriott of Marriott hotels, says the key to his organization's success is creating satisfied customers *and* satisfied employees. Marriott has found that happy, contented employees tend to treat customers better, which also increases the customers' satisfaction with the hotels.[7]

Your practice might consider providing an employee lunch room with microwave, refrigerator, table, and chairs. Furnishings should be attractive rather than cast-off items rejected by the local thrift store. Employees need to get away from the stress of the work environment during the day. If they have a comfortable and pleasant place to go, they'll be more likely to return to their jobs with a positive and client-pleasing attitude.

Attending to Special Populations

According to J. Jasinowski:

> *Our economic success depends on the benefits of diversity. Diversity brings a widened pool of talent, creativity and experience.... Given the demographic realities of our time, we either embrace diversity or limit our capacity to grow.*[8]

The concept of treating people well applies to *all* people. The world is fast becoming a melting pot as international borders crumble and once-intact countries and communities assimilate new ways, new attitudes, and new looks. Add to this cultural and ethnic mix an older population that has physical impairments plus a federal law designed to allow access for people with disabilities and those with other impairments or special needs, and it's apparent that you can't afford to neglect special populations. How do you address language and cultural differences, as well as the associated veterinary needs and expectations? How does your practice welcome the 25-year-old athlete who happens to use a wheelchair to get around?

When all staff members acknowledge the characteristics and needs of every individual as a unique person, they will provide truly personal service. You must know on a personal level what each individual wants and expects. Nowhere does this become clearer than where clients with ethnic, cultural, religious, social, physical, or age diversity are concerned.

Cultural and Ethnic Awareness

Obviously, you cannot turn a practice into a miniature United Nations of translators and ethnic/cultural anthropologists. If you often see clients of an ethnic or cultural group unfamiliar to you and your staff, however, you may need to invest in continuing education to familiarize everyone on the staff with the history, values, traditions, and beliefs of those groups.

Without acknowledgment and understanding of the cultural diversity of your clients, an essential element of client satisfaction—effective communication—can't take place. Communication entails more than words. For example, a certain amount of eye contact is considered a sign of mutual trust in mainstream American culture. In some other countries, though, direct eye contact is considered inappropriate. In some Arab and African cultures eye contact is prolonged to show interest, whereas many Americans would find lengthy eye contact uncomfortable.

Some ideas for learning about the ethnic and cultural beliefs of your clients are the following.

✦ Hire bilingual employees and employees who represent the ethnic or cultural group(s) you serve in your practice.

✦ Contact the language department or other appropriate department of a local community college or university to locate someone who is familiar with the cultural differences and influences of a specific ethnic group in your service area. Invite this expert to present an educational seminar for your practice veterinarians and staff.

✦ Recruit volunteers who are knowledgeable in the language and culture of ethnic or racial groups in your community.

Disability Awareness and Etiquette

The 1991 Americans with Disabilities Act (ADA) specifies certain modifications that businesses must make. An enlightened attitude about disabilities of any kind is equally important. Figure 2.1 will help you evaluate your approach to people with disabilities.

The staff in practices with a significant number of elderly clients can learn the special needs of this demographic group by experiencing them personally. An eye-opening role play involves simulating the physical limitations of advanced age. In this exercise staff members attempt to navigate the reception and exam areas while wearing ear plugs and petroleum-jelly-smeared glasses and wrapping their elbows, knees, and hands to restrict mobility. By experiencing the effects of cataracts, hearing loss, and arthritis, staff members begin to understand why Mr. Leebov doesn't follow the instructions you gave for treating his dog or why he looks on blankly as soft-spoken Robert, the veterinarian's assistant, explains pre-anesthetic procedures.

People with disabilities don't want pity; they want access and awareness. The ADA protects the civil rights of all individuals with disabilities and provides for access to the public as well as to employees of an organization. It mandates sensitivity to and accessibility for people with disabilities. You can't afford to fall short in this area, from both a legal and a client satisfaction perspective. A practice with 25 employees or more is required to make reasonable accommodations for employees with disabilities. Public access refers to the right of your clients and visitors who have physical or mental conditions or disabilities to be served in an equal and integrated manner.

This right to public access means that a veterinary practice, regardless of size, must:

Figure 2.1 Checklist for Satisfying Elderly and Disabled Clients

Use these questions as a checklist to evaluate how well your practice meets the needs of elderly and disabled.

✔ Do all staircases have handrails?

✔ Is the building easily accessible for cane, walker, and wheelchair users?

✔ Is the signage (exterior and door) visible, legible, and readable?

✔ Is the door to your clinic easy to open?

✔ Is there a clear path from the doorway to the reception desk?

✔ Do your chairs have straight arms and firm cushions?

✔ Is the lighting in your waiting room adequate for easy reading without causing glare?

✔ Is the type on your client information form large and easy to read?

✔ Is your bathroom well marked? Is it easy to get to? Does the door open without difficulty? Does it allow enough room to accommodate a walker or a wheelchair? Are there grab bars? Is the sink low enough?

✔ Does the reception area include a seat near the receptionist?

✔ Do staff members shout at the elderly to be heard, or do they use a slightly raised voice and enunciate clearly while looking directly at elderly persons to ensure understanding?

✔ Does the reception desk area have an area for clients to place personal belongings, and a leash hook or holding pen to restrain their pets while they're conducting business?

✔ Can all signs be read easily?

✔ Are educational materials readable by clients who have poor vision?

◆ Do those things that are "readily achievable" to eliminate architectural barriers.

◆ Meet the communication needs of persons with vision, hearing, and other impairments.

◆ Train staff members to provide service to clients with disabilities in a sensitive, respectful, and appropriate manner.

◆ Provide necessary aids, and modify policies, practices, and procedures as appropriate.

Complying with the ADA is important not only because it is a legal requirement but also because doing so (and perhaps doing more than the law requires) provides physical evidence of the commitment of a practice to its clients—all of them. Veterinarians and staff alike should be educated to dispel misconceptions and inaccuracies. At the same time, physical and attitude expectations of clients with disabilities should be clarified. One way to learn more is simply to ask people with disabilities what they want and expect—the same way you ask any of your clients those questions.

Ed and Toni Eames work to sensitize people about "disability-cool language." For instance, the term "Seeing Eye Dog" is a registered trademark and should be reserved for canine graduates of a specific school located in New Jersey. The term "guide dog" is preferred for general use. An entire chapter in the Eames's book *Partners in Independence: A Success Story of Dogs and the Disabled*[9] is devoted to veterinarians.

You may also have clients who are immune-compromised (those with AIDS, chemotherapy patients, and others). Can you answer their questions about appropriate precautions to take with their pets? Do you seek educational and conversational opportunities to ensure compassion and knowledge on the part of everyone in the practice?

Why are all these little details such a big deal? It's much easier to establish rapport with your clients if they are in a positive frame of mind. Although your interaction with them is important, it's only a fraction of what they experience when they visit your practice. Leverage the time you spend with your clients by making sure that every contact with your practice is as positive as it can be. Part of doing so is finding out what they want. The next chapter will show you how.

Notes

1. American Animal Hospital Association. *1995 AAHA Report: A Study of the Companion Animal Veterinary Services Market:* 75, 87, 105–106.
2. O. London. *Kill as Few Patients As Possible and 56 Other Essays on How To Be the World's Best Doctor.* Berkeley, CA: Ten-Speed Press, 1987: 5–6.
3. *1995 AAHA Report.*

Action Steps To Make a Positive First Impression

1. Promote a positive first impression of your practice by communicating your values to all support staff.

2. Make sure your practice is easy to find, and keep a high profile in your community.

3. Ensure that the staff handles payment questions tactfully.

4. Make "get-acquainted" appointments available to new clients, and send new-client information by mail before the first appointment.

5. Assess your hospital environment, inside and out, for cleanliness, accessibility, comfort, convenience, and appearance.

6. Provide the staff with a comfortable break/lunch room and restrooms.

7. If you have a client group with special requirements related to culture, ethnicity, disability, or age, make a sincere effort to learn about this group's needs, values, beliefs, and heritage.

6. Ashby. Practice Reflects a High Level of Care. *AAHA Trends*, Sep 1993:15–16.

7. S. Brown et al. *Patient Satisfaction Pays: Quality Service for Practice Success*. Gaithersburg, MD: Aspen Publications, 1993.

8. J. Jasinowski. Growth: The Imperative of Diversity in the 21st Century (Address to the Anti-Defamation League). *Vital Speeches of the Day* (Feb 1, 1998):92–95.

9. Eames, E, Eames, T. *Partners in Independence: A Success Story of Dogs and the Disabled*. New York: Howell Book House, 1997.

Chapter 3

Client Expectations

I expect my veterinarian to be good with my pet.

I want my veterinarian to treat me with respect.

I want a veterinarian who answers all my questions, someone I can trust with my pet.

What do clients want? This is a legitimate question, and not always an easy one to answer. Sometimes what they want isn't possible; financial constraints may limit or prevent providing what they, or even you, believe is best. Yet knowing what your clients want is the key to quality service; it paves the path to satisfaction.

Reasonable or Not?

Client satisfaction hinges on expectations. We know some things about what clients like: veterinarians who are good with pets, good with people, trustworthy, and knowledgeable.[1] What does that mean, specifically? It would certainly simplify matters if we could give you a Comprehensive Client Expectations Inventory that would allow you to predict exactly what questions or concerns you could anticipate. We can't give you a comprehensive list, though, because individual client expectations vary according to:

✦ age

✦ sex

◆ type of pet and its problem

◆ day of the week

◆ time of the day

◆ mood

◆ attitude

◆ the breakfast cereal he or she ate that day

You get the picture. Client expectations change, from one individual to another and even with the same client from one visit to another. But this doesn't get you off the hook. You must know what your clients expect, what they need, what they're concerned about. You need to know this before you depart the exam room and move on to another client, or how will you know whether you have met or surpassed the client's needs and expectations?

Importance of Client Expectations

Your client previews in his or her mind every "moment of truth" in the practice before the actual experience: the telephone appointment, the check-in at the front desk, the wait in the reception area, the technician's greeting, the interaction with the veterinarian, and any physical treatment or procedure that ensues. If your clients have unrealistic expectations and you do not gently realign them through education, they are likely to be disappointed when the mental movie they've created is overlaid with reality. This may affect their confidence in you and their willingness to follow prescribed treat-ment, to return for follow-up visits, and to recommend others to your practice.

More than half of pet owners have switched veterinar-ians at some point; 25% of those switched because of a bad experience.[2] Tops on the list of "bad experiences" were

◆ poor care

◆ dirty facilities

◆ unprofessional behavior

◆ inaccessibility

Although national surveys are helpful to gain the broad perspective, you need to know on a personal level what each of your clients wants and expects from you so that you and your staff can meet or manage these expectations. Knowing your clients' expectations helps you set standards—minimum daily service requirements—for the practice. You need to learn what your clients want and what they don't want, then act accordingly.

Personalizing Client Expectations

"Aha!" you say. "I get your point—I need to know what my clients want. Well, that's easy. I've seen articles describing what pet owners expect of their veterinarians. I'll refer to those."

That's a good idea. But don't stop there. Those thousands of pet owners are not clients in *your* practice. What each of your individual clients wants and expects from you and your staff is what counts, no matter how many pollsters with their pencils come knocking at the door.

"In our hospital, the doctors always take the history from the client themselves," says Dr. Robert Cartin. "I get nonverbal cues from the clients at that time, to help me understand exactly what they expect."

With appropriate questioning, probing, and other techniques, you and your staff can determine what each individual wants and needs. As you do, you'll note some similarities among age groups, men compared with women, and clients whose pets share similar diseases or problems. You'll also find disparities.

You can't generalize client expectations. That's why you need to bring client wants and needs to the personal level—a Gallup poll of one client. Your knowledge and experience allow you to make some general assumptions about diabetic patients, but to treat 10-year-old Snowball, a finicky feline, you must ask Sidney Burns, her owner, specific questions about his ability to administer daily injections, to change the cat's diet, and other matters. Your years of practice experience allow you to make some generalizations about what clients expect. Nevertheless, *this* client has specific expectations that you need to understand if you and your staff are to provide optimum service.

For example, Sidney may expect to be called Mr. Burns. He may expect a detailed explanation of your treatment protocol for diabetes. He may expect that you will lecture him about Snowball's diet. He may expect your clinic to be open early in the morning or late in the day to accommodate people who work. By knowing these expectations, you and your staff can strive to achieve them or discuss with Mr. Burns alternative ways to satisfy his needs.

A Few Generalizations

Now that we've convinced you that client expectations are personal, let's look at some generalizations that can be made about the most clients' expectations (we'll take a detailed look at each point in later chapters):

✦ Clients want personal concern. They want to feel that during the time you spend with their pets, that is the only thing that matters to you.

✦ Pet owners want complete medical records for their pets; consistency of care is important.

✦ Your clients want information about their pet's condition and treatment. They want this personally from you and your staff, and they also want something to review with family members.

✦ People expect you to honor their appointment times. If an emergency disrupts the schedule, they appreciate being informed about the estimated delay and given options if they can't or don't want to wait.

✦ Pet owners rank emergency service and extended hours as the most important services beyond veterinary medical and surgical care.[3]

✦ Clients want you to communicate with them in everyday language (no veterinary jargon; or, if veterinary terms are necessary, translate them).

✦ Your clients want a role in the interaction. They want you to ask them for their opinion and then to give them time to voice it. They want time to ask questions and to have their questions answered.

Tools for Measuring Clients Expectations

Like any business, large or small, a veterinary practice can't expect to achieve consistent, continued improvement and customer satisfaction without consistent, continued monitoring. What are we doing right? What needs to be fixed? What do our clients need, want, and think of us? Every practice should ask these questions in a number of formal, reliable, trackable ways.

As Peters and Waterman point out in *In Search of Excellence*,[4] effective service organizations have a remarkable people orientation, active involvement of senior management, and a high intensity of measurement and feedback. One, some, or all of the techniques that follow can help you and your staff discern client needs and concerns on an immediate, "this visit" basis as well as over the long term. At the same time, by determining expectations, you're conveying personal concern to your clients. You're letting them know, "I care about you. It's important to me that we know what you want and need."

Staff Discussion and Review

At the beginning or end of each day, gather your staff to go over the upcoming day's schedule. Review specific client's concerns, medical procedures that will be done, pending laboratory tests, and the treatment and evaluation plans for in-hospital patients. Get together at breakfast or lunch to share ideas and observations about individual clients and clients in general. Bring up client attitudes, concerns, complaints, and compliments, and come up with ways for veterinarians and staff to better understand and meet client needs.

Pre-Appointment "Prying"

Train your telephone receptionists to ask specific, detailed questions about the client's complaint or reason for the appointment. This "prying" enables them to know the client's specific concern so the proper amount of time is allotted (see Chapter 12). In return, you can let clients know what to expect by sending an information sheet before the first appointment, explaining the philosophy of your practice.

New Client Information Form

New client information forms should solicit more than just the required name, address, and phone number. Ask about all the pets in the household, number of children, if any, and the best days and times for appointments. Inquire about the client's previous veterinarian, and the reason for the switch.

Include a question that probes expectations such as, "What do you hope to gain from your appointment today?" or "What can Dr. Goodhealth and her staff do to meet your pet's health care needs?"

Some clinics ask their clients how they view their pets: as family members, or "just an animal." Pet owners may be divided into three categories: those who view their pets as children (70%), the practical pet owner (11%), and those who think the pet is "just an animal" (12%). Those who view their pets as children or who are "practical pet owners" visit the veterinarian more often; the "pets as children" group are older, spend significantly more money on their pets, and are less likely to have children of their own.[1]

Asking about a pet's origins may also reveal the type of bond between a pet and its owner. Was it wanted, received, the object of compassion (stray), or functional (for hunting/protection)? The source of a cat (but not a dog) influences the level of veterinary care sought, with cats acquired as strays receiving far less care.[1]

Others query their clients about their attitude toward spending money on the pet, giving choices ranging from "I'd max out my credit card to treat this pet," to "I really love my pet, but I have financial obligations, so there is a limit to what I can afford," to "if my pet develops a severe disease, the reality is that we'd not want to do anything extensive."

If you do this, consider it a general guideline only, and always ask the question again when a pet needs more than routine care. Remember that client needs and desires may change.

Figure 3.1 Post-Visit Survey Card

1. How long did you wait in the reception area? _____

2. Did you consider the waiting time: ❑ Brief ❑ Reasonable ❑ Excessive

3. Were you treated courteously by all staff members? _____

4. Was the doctor knowledgeable? _____

5. Was the doctor able to explain everything to your satisfaction? _____

6. Was the doctor friendly? _____

7. Did the doctor spend enough time with you? _____

8. Would you recommend this practice to others? _____

9. Do you have any suggestions for improving our practice? _____

Client Goals

Ask clients, "What is your goal for this visit?" At the end of the visit, ask, "What else do we need to discuss today?" If the client brings up another major problem that doesn't need immediate attention, let him or her know that you're concerned and that you want to take adequate time to address it. Say something like this: "Let's schedule an appointment for next week, when we can talk specifically about that. I want to give your pet's problem the time it deserves."

When treating a pet, emphasize that you are interested in the outcome: "We'll call you in a day or two to find out if you have any questions or are having any problems. If not, we'll see you next week to make sure the ear infection is under control."

Post-Visit Card

The doctor (for best response rate) or the receptionist can give each client a brief five- or six-question survey card after the visit. The client is encouraged to complete it in the clinic and then drop it in a sealed box in the reception area. Or the card can be prestamped so the client can fill it out at home and mail it back. A sample card is seen in Figure 3.1.

Client Questionnaires

Client questionnaires are probably the most-used way to measure and monitor the results of, and satisfaction with, the service and care offered by a practice. Dr. Gary Johnson of Dana Niguel Veterinary Hospital provides a form at the check-out counter for clients to fill out and mail to a third party "so that if they have something bad to say, they don't have to say it directly to us." Surveys must ask specific questions to get usable answers. Dr. Cartin initially used a survey that yielded positive answers to every question. "We now use a survey that is more in-depth," he said.

Dr. Thomas Austin of Newport Harbor Animal Hospital conducts monthly surveys of all the practice's new clients as well as a cross section of the existing client base. "Also, if we purge files, we survey the applicable clients before purging them," he said.

To gain insights into client expectations, include a question on your client survey such as: "Would you want to see this veterinarian again in the future? Why or why not?"

Client survey forms are available from the AAHA and the AVMA.[7] Use these standard forms or create a unique form that is best suited to your practice. Figures 3.2 and 3.3 provide examples.

A survey implies that you plan to fix what's wrong and to improve whatever clients rate as only "acceptable." Don't implement any form of survey unless you intend to act on the findings. Once implemented, a client survey provides a baseline against which future surveys (and the success of new service measures) can be evaluated.

Suggestion Box

It's an ancient idea, but suggestion boxes still work. Put a suggestion box in your reception area, put one in each exam room, and put cards nearby. A postcard format allows clients to write down their comments at home and mail them in. Post a sign, or print on the cards, "Please tell us what we're doing right and what we can do better." Act on every suggestion, and when clients sign their names, respond personally to thank them and

Figure 3.2 AAHA'S Client Survey

Client Survey

Thank you for giving us the opportunity to serve you. Please help us better meet your needs by taking a moment to complete this questionnaire, and returning it to the receptionist or mailing it to our office.

	Yes	No
1. Was your call answered promptly?.	☐	☐
2. Was our telephone response courteous and helpful?.	☐	☐
3. Was our waiting room comfortable and clean?.	☐	☐
4. Did your wait before seeing the doctor seem brief?	☐	☐

If not, how can we improve?_____

_____

_____

5. Was the veterinary technician helpful and careful with your pet?.	☐	☐
6. Was the doctor courteous and genuinely concerned with your pet's health?	☐	☐
7. Did the veterinarian explain your pet's problem clearly and completely?.	☐	☐
8. Do you feel your pet received quality professional health care?.	☐	☐
9. Did you find the facility clean?	☐	☐
10. If your pet was hospitalized, did the stay seem reasonable for the illness?	☐	☐
11. After a hospital stay, was your pet returned to you clean?	☐	☐
12. Was our payment policy clearly communicated to you?.	☐	☐
13. Was the billing presented in adequate detail?.	☐	☐
14. Would you recommend our veterinary practice to your friends?.	☐	☐
15. If your pet was groomed here, were you pleased?	☐	☐

16. Comments that you feel would help our practice _____

_____

_____

_____

Date service provided _____

Your name (optional) _____

Pet's name (optional) _____

#217   10/97 ©1997 AAHA Printed in the USA

Figure 3.3 Client Survey – Animal Hospital of Worthington

The doctors and staff of Animal Hospital of Worthington care about animals and their owners. We continually strive to give you and your pet the best quality service and attention possible. Please tell us how we are doing by completing this card and mailing it back to us. We really want to hear from you.

Date of Service: _____

IMPORTANCE TO YOU:

	VERY IMPORTANT	IMPORTANT	NOT VERY IMPORTANT
Quality of care for your pet.	☐	☐	☐
Length of waiting time at Hospital.	☐	☐	☐
Courtesy & professionalism of staff.	☐	☐	☐
Time to get an appointment.	☐	☐	☐
Value received for cost of service.	☐	☐	☐
Cleanliness and comfort of Hospital.	☐	☐	☐

HOW WE DID:

	EXCELLENT	AVERAGE	POOR	DON'T KNOW
Quality of care for your pet.	☐	☐	☐	☐
Length of waiting time at Hospital.	☐	☐	☐	☐
Courtesy & professionalism of staff.	☐	☐	☐	☐
Time to get an appointment.	☐	☐	☐	☐
Value received for cost of service.	☐	☐	☐	☐
Cleanliness and comfort of Hospital.	☐	☐	☐	☐

Comments: _____

How can we better serve you? _____

You may have a friend or acquaintance who might benefit from Animal Hospital of Worthington services. We'll be pleased to send them information: (Please provide name, address, phone number, and type of service.)

_____

_____

_____

(Following is optional)

YOUR NAME: Mr./Ms. _____
Mrs./Miss

Thank you!

Courtesy of Dr. George Norris and The Animal Hospital of Worthington. This survey is made as a postcard.

let them know what you've done in response to their suggestions.

At Broadway Animal Hospital in El Cajon, CA, staff members are encouraged to use a suggestion box. No matter how far-fetched, every idea is discussed and given consideration. When a staff member's idea is implemented, the result is satisfaction for staff and client alike.[8]

Telephone Surveys

Telephone surveys may reveal information not generated by written questionnaires. In a study developed by the University of California's Family Practice Clinic, researchers telephoned patients and asked them the same questions used on a written patient-satisfaction questionnaire. The telephone surveyors probed for clarification of patients' responses and often found that a person's initial response did not match the open-ended discussion that followed.

For example, a patient responded "extremely well" to the question, "How well does your doctor answer your questions?" Probing revealed the complaint that the physician often ignored the patient's questions or answered with "big words" she couldn't understand. Although praising the "excellent care" they received, most patients had at least one complaint about service, communication, convenience, or other surrogate indicators of care.[9]

Does this mean that written questionnaires are useless? No. Telephone interviews, however, can elicit clarification and detail regarding specific issues, new services, and potential trends identified through other monitoring techniques. Telephone surveys serve the same function as focus groups and other qualitative market research techniques: They add depth and substance to the statistics and data of written surveys.

Focus Groups and Client Councils

The focus group, once the domain of high-powered, high-cost market research firms, has taken a seat in veterinary practice. Although formal market research calls for a precise and structured method of conducting a focus group, you can use the concept less formally in your practice to determine what clients need and want.

For instance, you could gather half a dozen clients twice a year for an evening discussion of their fears, uncertainties, grievances, and needs. These sessions may heighten clients' expectations and understanding of their responsibilities. Use an objective moderator who spends more time listening than talking, asking questions such as: "What do you feel makes a good doctor?" and "What are your biggest concerns when you drop off your pet for surgery?" Make a videotape or an audiotape for later review by veterinarians and staff members. That can provide compelling evidence of the need for change in attitude or behavior within the practice.

One meeting could focus on the idea of "walking through" a typical client visit. List each step, and ask clients how they would like the interaction to transpire and what behaviors, words, and attitudes would represent a maximum service level.

Another option is to form a client council—a group of clients who present their ideas, complaints, concerns, and suggestions for improvement. The council would meet three or four times a year, and discussion topics could be random or specific (particularly if an issue has been identified in the practice as affecting service quality). Rotate the council membership to ensure an infusion of new perspectives.

If you conduct focus groups or form a client council, keep in mind this unbreakable rule: Implement recommendations when you can, and follow up with the client(s) on those you can't. If no action results from clients' input, you'll lose credibility (and clients).

Evaluation of Referral Veterinarians

When you send a client to a specialist, ask the client about his or her perception of that veterinarian, the staff, and the visit. Before referring clients, find out whether the specialist has a veterinary care philosophy similar to yours. Determine this before sending a client to that specialist, if possible. Discuss with clients not only the reason for a referral but also what to expect. Clients will judge you according to the quality and service provided by the veterinarians to whom you send them. This veterinarian's story may strike a familiar chord with you:

> I'm glad when specialists are nice, but I always refer on ability to get the job done. The best internist here can have a great attitude or she can be quite offensive. I first try to assess the clients with respect to their likely reaction to either end of her spectrum. If the situation warrants, either due to the pet's condition or the client's sensitivity, I will simply offer to take the pet to see her myself. If I think a client can handle her (the pet's condition often has a bearing on this too), I'll say that she is the best diagnostician and ultrasonographer, and that I think she is the most likely to figure out what is going on with the pet as well as provide the best treatment plan. I warn them to be prepared for her attitude to be unpleasant or standoffish. The interesting thing is that ever since I've sent people to her with this warning, I've had nothing but glowing reports of her attitude and behavior.

If you're on the other end of that relationship—your practice *sees* pets referred by other veterinarians—keep in mind that the pet owner *and* the referring veterinarian are both important customers. You may wonder, "What can a survey of referring veterinarians tell me about client expectations?" You might be surprised. Clients often report back to the veterinarian who referred them (and the savvy referring veterinarian solicits feedback) to say, "Dr. Gottlieb really knew his stuff, but I wish he had given me a pamphlet or something about the surgery. I didn't really understand some of what he was saying, so I couldn't explain it to my wife." Use a well-structured survey to find out what referral sources and their clients say about you. Knowing referral source opinions and needs is another way to reassure clients of the continuity of care and communication between you and their primary veterinarian.

Dr. Suann Hosie is head of Vancouver Animal Emergency Clinic, a 24-hour critical care facility in Vancouver, British Columbia. She recognizes the challenge of having two clients to nurture: the pet owner and the referring veterinarian. Dr. Hosie's team keeps the primary veterinarian informed of changes in the pet's condition. Together, the pet owner, the critical care veterinarian, and the primary-care veterinarian make decisions regarding continued care.[10]

Ongoing Monitoring

There you have it—an assortment of techniques for determining, anticipating, and monitoring your clients' expectations. You can't satisfy your clients if you don't know what they're looking for. Talking to and listening to your clients in a variety of ways is the only means of understanding and meeting their needs and, ultimately, surprising them by surpassing their expectations.

Monitoring client satisfaction requires subsequent action and change. Clients expect it. It's implied in the process of seeking opinions (why else would you do it?). If veterinarians or their staffs are not committed to quality service and do not believe strongly in and reveal quality service attitudes, clients won't believe the results of any monitoring or evaluation efforts.

Says Dr. George Norris:

If you ask for comments, use the information. If clients complain and give their names, you must let them know that their complaints were heard and you are working on solutions. If clients take the trouble to complain and then feel ignored, they will undoubtedly feel angry.[11]

A significant challenge with practices in which veterinarians haven't accepted a customer-first philosophy is resistance by these veterinarians to the results. Some may argue that the data are invalid. If you encounter this problem, go back to Chapter 1. You *must* achieve participation and involvement. Everyone must believe that quality counts and that clients come first. You must commit to your belief and then measure expectations, monitor the results, and act on what you learn.

Think of monitoring quality service efforts as "service recall." You do it with your clients routinely. If you diagnose a Springer Spaniel with acute purulent otitis, you'll probably prescribe a course of treatment and ask

Action Steps for Measuring and Monitoring Client Expectations

1. Understand that client expectations change, and maintain a flexible attitude.

2. Recognize that clients expect a personal relationship that shows compassion and caring.

3. Find out what your clients want and what they don't want. Ask questions, and listen attentively to their answers.

4. Obtain client feedback via a number of different means to get the best results.

5. Implement at least one formal, comprehensive process for determining client satisfaction, and repeat it regularly so improvements or problems can be tracked.

6. Once a process is in place, incorporate follow-up—the action that will take place and the individual responsible for it—when problems are identified.

7. Gently manage unrealistic expectations through client education.

8. Use your staff to help you uncover things that are going on in a client's life. Encourage staff members to verbalize their observations and ideas.

the clients to bring in the dog for a follow-up visit in a week. You want to make sure the treatment is working.

Formal client satisfaction monitoring is the means by which you make sure the service "treatment" is working in your practice. It's service follow-up. You evaluate satisfaction to be certain that the service you offer is accomplishing your objectives and meeting or surpassing client expectations. When you evaluate results and measure them against standards or goals, you know whether you're successful.

Notes

1. American Animal Hospital Association. *1995 AAHA Report: A Study of the Companion Animal Veterinary Services Market*, 35: 81–97.
2. *1995 AAHA Report.*
3. *1995 AAHA Report.*
4. T. J. Peters and R. H. Waterman, Jr. *In Search of Excellence: Lessons from America's Best-Run Companies.* New York: Harper & Row, 1982: 249.

5. *1995 AAHA Report.*

6. *1995 AAHA Report.*

7. D. Scott. *Client Satisfaction: The Other Half of Your Job.* Menlo Park, CA: Crisp Publications/AVMA, 1991: 102–103.

8. A. Ashby. Communication is Key to This Practice's Success. *AAHA Trends,* May 1993:15–16.

9. Goldsmith GA. Patient Satisfaction with a Family Practice Clinic: Comparison of a Questionnaire and an Interview Survey. *Journal of Ambulatory Care Management,* May 1983: 24–31.

10. R. Hawn. The Evolution from All-night Emergency to 24-hour Critical Care. *AAHA Trends,* Sep 1995:13–15.

11. H. Trux and G. Norris. Bottoms Up, Everybody! *AAHA Trends* Apr/May, 1993: 26–27.

Chapter 4

What Clients Want to Know

[Doctors] toss about specialized terminology the way a cook flips hamburgers at a fast-food restaurant, neglecting to translate acronyms or explain procedures. . . ."[1]—Paul Rousseau, MD

Veterinarians and physicians have in common the challenge of communicating professional concepts so clients can understand them. Rousseau recognizes that communication and education are often more important in ensuring quality care than the medical lingo, fancy gadgets, and high-tech tests and procedures to which health professionals sometimes are wedded.

Today's clients want information, education, and a complete understanding of their pets' condition and treatment. They equate communication with quality. Are you giving them the information they want, in a way they understand?

Client education is critical to compliance and outcome, and it satisfies client expectations. Education provides the following benefits:

✦ Information gives your message a consistent quality.

✦ Client education provides tangible evidence of the visit and minimizes liability.

✦ Informed clients make educated decisions and are more compliant.

✦ Informed clients are more confident in their veterinarian.

✦ Clients look to their veterinarian as a primary source of information.

One survey revealed that clients prefer to spend 11 to 20 minutes in the exam room.[2] They want information, but they're busy, too. How long is your typical exam—10 minutes, or 20? That's only a fraction of the time your clients spend living with their pets' conditions. You can't go home with every client, but you can help clients understand how to make decisions so they can have some independence in their pets' care.

Benefits of Education for Veterinarian *and* Client

Although education takes time, it saves time in the end. Veterinarians who take the time to review lab tests, diagnoses, and treatments with their clients and give them information to take with them report that their clients require less follow-up time on the phone and in the office. Taking the time to discuss your findings and your diagnostic or treatment plan with your clients indicates that you respect them enough to take the time to talk with them and that you think they are intelligent enough to understand.

Veterinarians should avoid making assumptions about their clients' level of knowledge or their ability to apply it under stress. Professionals in the human medical field require educating just as your other clients do. One gynecologist's dog developed renal failure after her attempt to treat its arthritis with high doses of ibuprofen. In another case, a surgeon tried to treat his dog for vomiting and loose stools for two weeks with drugs labeled for human use. Dr. Mike Bellinghausen of Kenmore, WA, recalls, "He finally brought it in late on a Saturday afternoon, and we ended up going to surgery to remove some underwear from the intestine."

The veterinarian doesn't have to do all the educating. Many of the veterinarians with whom we spoke acknowledged that clients often hesitate to bring up questions for fear of appearing "stupid." These veterinarians review the problem and proposed treatment with the client, then turn him or her over to a technician who is trained to give in-depth information and to probe for underlying concerns.

Decreased Liability

Education instills confidence in your clients, and what's more (there's no doubt about it), education limits malpractice liability. It's a quantifiable and tangible component of communication that more and more clients expect.

The concept of informed consent is difficult for some veterinarians to put in writing. Somehow, that piece of paper seems too formal or too much trouble. Perhaps these veterinarians think that telling clients of the risks involved in some procedures will only scare them away. Just ask veterinarians who use consent forms, though, and you'll find that they are pleased with the results.

For example, veterinarians who recommend pre-anes-thetic blood tests use a consent form that lists the reasons for those tests and the risks of not having them done. The client's signature acknowledges in writing that he or she understands these risks and benefits. Asking for clients' signatures makes them realize that you're serious about having them understand what's involved, and may prompt them to ask additional questions about the procedure that they would not have asked otherwise.

Using client educational materials addresses the client's "need to know" as well as the legal requirement for informed consent:

✦ It is a visual presentation that helps clients understand what they will experience.

✦ It is reproducible evidence.

✦ It is documentable. Consent forms are filed in the client's record along with a notation of which video the client was shown or brochure they received.

Legal consent forms are available from a variety of sources, including the AAHA and the AVMA.

Increased Client Satisfaction

Once again we can learn from physicians' experience: Information increases client satisfaction even when the news is not good. In one study, two specialists in Australia sent cancer patients a letter summarizing what had been discussed during their initial visit, including treatment choices, test results, status of the disease, and referral arrangements. Patients who got the letter of explanation rated their overall satisfaction as higher than those who didn't. They also said they remembered what they had been told and that they had a chance to ask all the questions they wanted.[3]

Educational materials for clients provide tangible evidence of the visit and your service quality. Educational information—whether in the form of a computer-printed information sheet developed in the office, a custom-printed brochure, a purchased information pamphlet, an audiocassette, a video, a hand-drawn illustration, or a formal, structured class or educational session—demystifies and personalizes veterinary care. It provides tangible evidence that you are concerned and that you want your client to be informed. It is an after-the-visit reminder of the quality of service you provided.

Dr. Thomas Austin agrees, with this caveat: "Any information our clients take home is just reinforcement. We want them to understand what we're talking about when they walk out the door."

Informed Decisions

Encouraging questions helps clients make informed decisions. Pet owners don't always know or think of the right questions when they are in the veterinarian's exam room. Anxiety, stress, and the "white coat syndrome" fog some people's thinking.

"Ask clients if they have any questions before they leave the exam room, but be sure you aren't halfway out the door when you ask," writes Kathy Czepiel. "If you are, they'll get the message that you really don't want them to ask you anything."[4]

"I've found the toughest clients are those who don't say a lot in the exam rooms—basically quiet people," says

Dr. Bellinghausen. "With these clients you often make assumptions, which may be wrong or right."

Despite everything we've said about clients as consumers, about clients who stand up to their veterinarians and demand complete detailed explanations, a certain number of clients will meekly accept what they are told; they will not question or press for details, and they will leave your practice without a clear understanding of what they have been told or what they have been instructed to do.

Some clients are uninformed about what signs or conditions require professional care, when self-care and over-the-counter medications are advisable, and so forth. And some simply don't know how to carry out the instructions you've given them.

How do you get passive clients to participate? These people will benefit from additional information they can take home to review with family members. They are more likely to follow instructions because they are more likely to understand them. Clients will make better decisions about diet, exercise, medications, and follow-up care if you:

✦ Explain why over-the-counter medications for humans aren't safe for pets.

✦ Educate them about signs their pets might show that suggest a call to the veterinarian.

✦ Give them information about small things they can do themselves before they call you (take the pet's temperature, look at the color of its gums, etc), to help them decide whether the situation is urgent.

Helping clients assume their role in the pet's health care partnership sometimes takes prompting. Uninformed clients whose pets have had surgery are a particular concern, as appropriate home care is essential. If a client doesn't seem to understand the scheduled procedure, explain it in more detail. This special attention increases efficiency while enhancing client satisfaction because it reduces the chance of getting a phone call the next day that takes staff members or veterinarians away from other tasks.

At the Animal Health Centre in Fresno, California, hospital director Dr. Lee Ann DuMars insists that her staff demonstrate or explain at-home care procedures at the time of an animal's discharge. Clients then are asked to repeat the procedure to demonstrate that they can do it. From ear cleaning to replacing bandages, this ensures client comprehension, and it lets the staff see and develop better strategies for challenges such as a particularly wiggly pet.[5]

Compliance and Understanding

"Why should I pay for procedures or medication for my pet to treat a disease whose signs I haven't noticed and that isn't bothering my pet?" asks an Oregon pet owner.

Why, indeed? It's up to you to explain why early heart or kidney disease may require a change in the pet's diet or medication to prevent it from worsening. Don't blame your client for having a hard-headed attitude.

How often have you had a client stop using medication when the pet's problem appeared to clear up? These clients obviously don't realize that the treatment may fail when it is not completed as instructed. Of course, this points to the significance of good communication about the purpose of the medication and the importance of completing it.

At the Animal Health Centre, a technician performs a pre-doctor interview of each client. If the pet is obese, needs dental prophylaxis, or is showing signs of behavior problems, the technician will discuss options with the client. "This gives them a chance to hear it from the technician before they hear it from me," says Dr. DuMars. "By the time I go in, I'm just reinforcing."[6]

At the end of the appointment, Dr. DuMars asks clients whether they have any questions and whether they are comfortable with the plan. She points out that if clients disagree with your plan, they probably won't ask questions.

A Source of Information

Your clients need to be taught that when they want information, your clinic is the place to get answers. Make sure your receptionist doesn't draw a blank when asked about house calls, puppy training classes, boarding facilities, or grooming services. *If you don't offer those services, be sure you can direct your clients to someone who can.* An added benefit of referrals to other businesses is the return referrals they send to you.

Although newspapers, general-interest magazines, and pet-care publications are common sources of knowledge about new developments in the world of veterinary medicine, clients still turn to their veterinarians as the ultimate credible authority. Magazines, newspapers, and the evening news are impersonal and nonspecific, and they raise further questions that need personalized answers. When Frances, your client, reads in the latest issue of *Cat Fancy* about a new leukemia test, she looks to you to personalize what she has read.

Giving clients a personal response need not require a lengthy discourse. Printed information can back up a brief explanation from the veterinarian, yet still appear personalized. In computerized practices, clearly written descriptions of the most commonly treated conditions and treatment options can be stored on the computer. The veterinarian can then note on the chart which information form should be printed out for the client.

Because people want information about the latest veterinary care trends, it's a good idea to subscribe to the most popular pet magazines and newspapers for exam rooms as well as the reception area. Both national and local publications (such as your local Cat Club Newsletter) should be included. A staff member should be given the responsibility of reviewing these publications as they arrive and alerting the veterinarian to articles or news reports that may generate client comments or questions. Some practices prepare scrapbooks of articles from newspapers and magazines on veterinary subjects of interest to clients.

In some cases it is wise to plan ahead and develop a written response or position paper for controversial articles. Cornell University's Feline Health Center responded to concerns about vaccine-induced sarcomas by producing a brochure (also available from AAHA), "Feline Vaccines: Benefits and Risks." A similar brochure is available from the AVMA.

Printed materials, videos, audiocassettes, and other forms of client education provide a consistent message that can be documented. This also points out the importance of giving a consistent message about clinical policies and procedures to staff as well as to clients.

What methods work best? Clients report that their favorite educational and communication tools are brochures, anatomical drawings, in-clinic posters, and informational mailings.[7] It depends on the individual, so a combination of methods will ensure that you have a means of reaching every client.

We hear mixed results from veterinarians who use videotapes for client education. One thing is clear: Use of an infomercial-type video without personal input from a staff member is a waste of time. Targeted videos, such as those that outline the benefits and risks of certain surgical procedures, effectively educate clients about their pets' health care.

Educating Clients About Your Services

Are your clients aware of the *value* of the services you provide? Educating pet owners includes filling them in on the details of what you do. Do they know that you wear a cap, mask, and gown during surgery, and that you use the safest anesthetics available? Do they know what is involved in a "routine fecal?"

The *AAHA Report* revealed that 51% of pet owners are unsure whether their veterinarians offer access to a specialist; 48% are unaware of the availability of housecalls from their veterinarian; 26% don't know whether their vet offers grooming services; and 34% don't know whether dental services are available.[8]

"Dentistry has been our major marketing focus," comments Dr. Paul Glouton of Lilburn Animal Hospital in Lilburn, GA. "If that's true, what must our clients' perception be of our less visible services?"[9]

Are your clients aware that you consult with specialists, or that you have an ultrasound machine? Through tours and with pictures (in a clinic brochure, in your front office, and on your web site), show your clients what you do. Consider holding an open house so new clients—

and established ones—can take a fresh look at your facilities. Increasing clients' awareness of what you offer will increase their perception of the value of your services.

Making Client Education a Service Strategy

To incorporate client education into your service strategies, follow these steps:

1. Make a commitment to client education. Investigate sources for information that reflect your views and beliefs. AAHA, the AVMA, and others offer catalogs of educational materials. Pharmaceutical companies are a generous source of information (but be sure their material doesn't overemphasize the drug they're selling—you may have some lengthy explaining to do when you recommend a different treatment).

2. If what you find doesn't say what you want your clients to hear, write and print your own material. It doesn't have to be fancy, expensive, or elaborate. Many veterinarians prepare simple, typewritten instruction or information sheets to give to clients. Use language that your clients will understand, with words that create mental pictures, common terms, and analogies ("redness" instead of "erythema," "adrenal gland malfunction" instead of "hypoadrenocorticism").

3. Give clients information in print and pictures. Use anatomical drawings filled in with details specific to your client. Develop instruction sheets and descriptive forms.

4. Establish a standard and a protocol to be followed to be certain that every client gets accurate, detailed information pertaining to his or her pet's condition, treatment, surgery, or health status. Documentation of client education should always go in the veterinary record, of course, to improve compliance and to reduce liability. Client education protocols should include the following:

   ✦ When materials should be given (such as before a pet's scheduled surgery and when a condition is diagnosed)

◆ What the client is to receive

◆ Who should provide it

◆ The form or format in which the material should be provided (print, video, audio, personal explanation, etc.)

◆ What confirmation or follow-up is required (completion of a form by the client acknowledging receipt of the information, repetition of key information by the client to confirm understanding, a follow-up phone call by the veterinary assistant to ensure understanding, compliance)

◆ Documentation in the veterinary record

5. Educate clients before and after their visit to your clinic. Many hospitals use presurgical information forms as well as printed take-home instructions. AAHA's Presurgical Care form, shown in Figure 4.1, is an example of how you can help clients better understand what to expect. A standard consent form may be found in the AVMA *Membership Directory and Resource Manual*.

6. Don't let any client leave your clinic without tangible evidence of your commitment to education. Even (especially) clients whose pets are healthy can benefit from educational information. Develop a library of health and wellness material, and pass it out freely to every client. When you give someone a handout about the importance of weight reduction in obese pets, or about the signs to watch for in a geriatric pet, the subtle message is, "I care about you." This is a powerful, virtually unbreakable thread to weave through the fabric of the veterinarian-client relationship.

7. Use your staff to fill in the gaps. Many practices have a client coordinator, technician, or other employee who comes into the exam room when the veterinarian leaves, to answer client questions and provide detailed instructions. This can be more effective and more productive than relying on the veterinarian alone.

Figure 4.1 AAHA Presurgical Care Instruction Form

PRESURGICAL CARE

Patient_____ Date of Surgery___/ ___/ ___ Time _____

Please read and follow the steps outlined to prepare your pet for surgery. This information is provided with your pet's safety in mind.

No food after _____ am/pm the day of/before surgery.

No water or other liquids after _____ am/pm the day of/before surgery.

Drop off your pet by _____ am/pm on the day of surgery.

You may call after _____ am/pm to obtain your pet's condition and tentative release time.

____ Vaccinations are current until _____.

____ We have no record of your pet's vaccination (please bring proof).

HOSPITAL/SURGICAL INFORMATION

- Preparation — The skin surrounding the surgical area will be clipped and scrubbed with an antiseptic. Equipment used will be sterilized, and surgery personnel will antiseptically scrub and wear gloves, masks, gowns and caps during the operation.

- Anesthesia — Local or general anesthesia may be used. Some risk is involved, depending upon the general condition of your pet, age, etc. Surgery may occur as scheduled or be delayed, depending upon the determination after presurgical examination.

- Heart/Respiration — Monitoring of these functions will occur during the operation.

POSTSURGICAL CARE

Both staff and doctor will check your pet routinely during the hospital stay, and again just prior to discharge. We will meet with you before taking your pet home, and give you postsurgical information. If you wish to discuss this only with the doctor, please make advance arrangements.

#235   Copyright © 1990 AMERICAN ANIMAL HOSPITAL ASSOCIATION   1/90

Educating clients keeps them coming back. One veterinarian attaches a "client education list" to every new puppy or new kitten record. The list includes nutrition, behavior, skin care, and similar information. At each visit for booster vaccinations or deworming, one or more of the subjects is discussed with the client and checked off the list. This approach ensures that every client hears all the information, divided into easily digestible portions.

Meeting Client Needs

Contrary to many veterinarians' fears, educated clients won't begin to "be their own veterinarians." As one veterinarian noted, "The more knowledgeable my clients become the more they contact me with interesting questions and the quicker they are to call when something is amiss."

Asking clients what they want, need, and expect, and then educating them about your services and care of their pets, does more than meet the client's needs. It gives your practice a marketing edge. The more clients know about the services you offer and the conditions you treat, the more they'll make use of your services. The more you know about their expectations, the better you can serve their needs.

Notes

1. P. A. Rousseau. A Painful Lack of Education. *Patient Care*, Sept 30, 1990: 32.
2. W. Myers. What Do Clients Want? *Veterinary Economics*, June 1997: 40–52.
3. E. Bishop. Doctors Get Results by Sending Letters After Treatment. *Wall Street Journal*, Oct 11, 1991: B-3.
4. K. L. Czepiel. They're Calling *Us*—Why Aren't They Asking *You? AAHA Trends*, Dec/Jan 1997: 19–20.
5. R. Hawn. *AAHA Trends*, Jan/Feb 1997: 24–25.
6. Hawn.
7. American Animal Hospital Association. *1995 AAHA Report: A Study of the Companion Animal Veterinary Services Market*: 100–101.
8. *1995 AAHA Report.*
9. Applying the Results from the AAHA Report. *AAHA Trends*, Dec/Jan 1996: 24–25.

Action Steps for Educating Clients

1. Establish a client education program in your practice to ensure that every client receives tangible information about his or her pet's health or condition.

2. Use consent forms to educate and minimize liability.

3. Purchase or prepare printed information about conditions you commonly treat, medications you prescribe, or routine surgical procedures.

4. Have a staff member review popular magazines for veterinary articles that may require written comment or elaboration for clients in your practice.

5. Recognize that people learn in different ways. Don't rely on only one medium; use print, models, videotapes, audiocassettes, drawings, and computer software.

6. Use everyday language that your clients can understand.

7. Don't make assumptions about a client's level of knowledge. Ask.

8. Investigate and use information available from the AVMA, AAHA, pharmaceutical companies, and other sources.

9. Don't forget your staff. They can fill in the blanks and often will elicit further questions and concerns that clients may hesitate to bring up to you.

10. Strive for understanding before the client leaves the clinic. Educational materials should be a back-up, not a substitute, for good communication.

Part Two

Teamwork Improves Client Satisfaction

Satisfying the client requires a team effort—but how will you get your team behind you? Start by embracing your role as leader. Effective leaders have a vision for their practices. We'll show you how to create your own vision, and then to set standards to ensure that your vision materializes.

What motivates people to rise to the challenge of performing at their best? Effective leaders know how to motivate and empower employees. You'll find that a satisfied team makes for satisfied clients.

Motivation can take you and your staff only so far, though. Without expertise and continuing education, your services will fall short. We'll show you how to keep yourself and your staff on top of the learning curve, including how to learn from and adapt the best and most appropriate strategies from other businesses—a process called *benchmarking*.

We know there are hospitals where the veterinarians are too busy or too distracted to give this book the attention it deserves. We realize that many readers are practice managers, so we've devoted an entire chapter to their unique viewpoint. As one of the leaders of the practice team, the practice manager can apply all the concepts we discuss and can help motivate the practice owner to join in the team effort toward improving client satisfaction.

Chapter 5

A Shared Vision

What you are speaks so loudly I cannot hear what you say.—Ralph Waldo Emerson

A leader can be defined as

1. A person who leads others along a way; a guide;

2. One in charge or in command of others.

Joel Barker, author of *Future Edge*, says a leader is "a person you will follow to a place you wouldn't go by yourself."[1] That's a pithy definition, and we would modify it: A leader is someone you'll follow. Period.

Leadership is an attribute and a skill, not a title. Every organization needs a *manager*—someone to ensure structure, continuity, and consistency, someone to maintain the framework. Every organization also needs a *leader*, someone its constituents follow confidently and in whom they believe. In some organizations the manager and the leader are the same person. Extremely fortunate organizations have more than one manager/leader. When the person who occupies the leader's position does not demonstrate leadership traits and actions, the group informally elevates or appoints someone to leadership status, or someone from within the group assumes the role by demonstrating the required leadership skills.

Veterinarians and practice managers must acknowledge and accept their role and responsibility as leaders. In doing this, they:

✦ are enthusiastic;

✦ make decisions, then explain them—before, during, or afterward, depending on the timing and circumstances;

✦ let others make decisions; give them authority and accountability;

✦ recognize the participation and contributions of others.

Showing What You Mean

Your staff members look to you for leadership, guidance, and vision. They listen intently to what you say, and they observe even more critically what you do. If your words and actions don't match, your staff will be confused. They may take their cue from your behaviors—the way you interact with clients, your colleagues, and other employees—rather than heed your words. A study by the American Society for Quality Control reported that employees perceive a gap between what CEOs say about quality as a company priority and what they actually do.[2] When words and deeds don't match, the deed is believed every time.

The veterinarian sets an example for the staff, making sure the people in the hospital observe how he or she handles different client personalities. For example, owners of dying pets may be angry and take it out on the staff. The leader explains to the staff that these pet owners aren't angry with the staff. They're dealing with a frightening diagnosis. "Their words or actions have nothing to do with us personally, so we shouldn't respond in anger or hostility, but with compassion."

Whether you are seen as the leader of the practice depends on:

✦ What you say (What are the words?)

✦ How you say it (What is your tone?)

✦ Whether you mean it (Are you sincerely committed?)

✦ How you act it out (Do your actions match your words?)

Listening and Trust

According to receptionist Carolyn Prusinski:

I know this sounds corny, but we work as a team. The doctors let the staff members do their jobs— they don't look over our backs. Everyone gives more than 100 percent, because we're allowed to. We're allowed to experiment, implement, and do our job. They trust us to do what we were hired to do.[3]

A leader instills action, continued innovation, and results by encouraging the growth of new leaders. This happens when staff members are given firm guidance, a voice in the action, and the information necessary to make knowledgeable decisions. Instead of simply observing problems, leaders lead others toward solutions. The smart doctor knows that staff members see and hear clients more than the doctor does. The staff thus can offer ideas and improvements that directly affect how clients view the practice.

Leaders seek, listen to, and implement the opinions and ideas of others. They recognize that the best ideas come from those who are engaged directly in a process. They encourage employees to listen to clients and to look for processes that can be improved. They listen to the receptionist who has an idea about changing the schedule, to the veterinary assistant who sees a better way to ensure client compliance, and to the client who thinks he or she doesn't have enough information about the antibiotics you've prescribed.

A leader allows others the possibility of making a mistake. Your staff needs to know that you, too, make mistakes. Initiating change in the practice is bound to produce missteps and errors at first. Service recovery, discussed in Chapter 15, helps you learn from mistakes. Through training and ongoing education, you can help staff avoid serious mistakes.

This is a big step, and a tough one for many veterinarians. It means giving your staff the latitude to make meaningful decisions. It means encouraging them to have impact in your practice. It means showing them that you have trust and confidence in them, starting with sharing your goals for the practice.

"Just do it" was Nike's slogan for the 1990s, urging people to quit contemplating fitness and to take action. This get-it-done approach may work fine for running, weight lifting, and aerobic exercise—and for selling shoes. When it comes to a long-term quality service strategy, though, "just doing it" without a little planning first may not be the most desirable way to achieve client satisfaction. Not if you want lasting results and employees who provide a high level of service along with you. In the following chapters we'll describe in detail how to empower your employees, delegate, and listen effectively. But first, you must have a *vision* in order to lead your team.

Sharing Your Vision

> *If you don't know where you're going, you might end up there.* —Yogi Berra

A vision gives you a sense of direction, a purpose, and a place to go. Defining and communicating a vision for your practice is like turning on the light after stumbling around a room in the dark. With the light out, you eventually may figure out how to get from one end of the room to the other, but only after stubbing your toe on the sofa, knocking over a lamp, and stepping on the cat's tail.

Nevertheless, many veterinarians, banded together in a group practice or making their way on their own, grope along in the dark. Perhaps defining a direction for the practice is made to seem like a mysterious, lengthy, and difficult task. Maybe you think it calls for a consultant (or a whole pack of them) to whisk you away to some expensive resort for three days of solemn talk, at the end of which you will have come up with a *vision* (bells ringing, horns blowing) designed to send you soaring into the future.

Guess what? You don't necessarily need a consultant (although a consultant or objective outside expert can be helpful in guiding and melding diverse points of view). And it shouldn't take three days to come up with a vision and goals for achieving the vision. What you need are:

✦ Some idea of your values—what's important to you in your practice and in serving your clients

✦ A sense of purpose (why you want to accomplish what you want to accomplish)

✦ Trust and confidence in those you've chosen to help you achieve your goals

✦ Realistic understanding of your personal and professional style—the way you work and play

✦ Understanding of the threats, opportunities, and trends that may affect how you practice medicine in the future.

Now you can examine your beliefs, attitudes, and core values for each of the points above and come up with written statements that clarify each point. If you've been in practice for some time, you may wish to do a little historical research first. What have your style, activities, and results been in the past? How have you behaved? Behavior is a reflection of belief. What changes or improvements do you plan, or wish, to make?

Gather the Troops and Get Their Ideas

At this point you can bring the staff together. If you have a group practice with a large staff, you may wish to select members to gather ideas and offer input on behalf of the whole group. Your staff members are your deputies, carrying out the quality mission along with you. You need to know what they are thinking and what their beliefs are as much as they need to know what you think and believe. Try to get away from the clinic. A meeting room at a local hotel or a community room of the library will work well. Close the practice at noon or all day, or devote a weekend afternoon to this discussion. If you ask your staff to give up free time, pay normal overtime rates. Say something like, "I need your help in moving into the future with the practice. We're going to take a look at where we've been and figure out where to go and how best to get there. You know our clients and my style and the problems and opportunities as well as I do—maybe better. Will you help me plan where we're going?"

The day arrives. The room is equipped with chairs comfortably grouped around a table. Refreshments are available in a corner of the room. You have a flipchart and marker pens, and you've designated a recorder (someone to take good notes from the discussion). Now your staff—two sets of eyes, or perhaps 10 or even 20— are focused eagerly on you.

To put things in perspective, start by recounting to your staff a history of the practice. It doesn't have to be long and detailed. Be upbeat and include anecdotes and humorous mistakes to make your history come alive and to help everyone understand your beliefs and values. This oral history will help those who are charged with moving you into the future understand how you and they have arrived at this point. If you have one or more longtime staff members, encourage them to help tell the history, particularly some of the significant highlights or amusing moments they recall.

Explain What You Believe and Why

In your review of the practice, explain (for a group practice, have a few veterinarians do this):

✦ Why you became a veterinarian

✦ Why you chose to work with the species you do

✦ What you like about veterinary medicine and your special areas of interest

✦ What you don't like about both

✦ What, if anything, you would change about your decisions regarding the focus of your practice, its location and environment, and type of animals and their owners you see

✦ What you hope to change or improve in the future

In doing this, you are giving your staff a sense of who you are and what you believe in. This may be hard for you. You may wonder, "What if I say too much? Too little? What if they think I'm self-indulgent or senti-mental? What if they don't understand why I'm telling this to them?"

Don't worry. If you explain your intentions ("We're going to create a quality road map for the practice"), your staff will appreciate and enjoy your review. Explain that it helps to know where you've been when you're planning a trip so you don't take the same detours and forks in the road and stop at the same bad roadside restaurants as the last time you made the trip.

When you've finished your history, you'll need to answer a few questions to develop a vision. For this you'll need your staff's input. A vision must be shared if it is to be believed and acted out. (It's that commitment thing again!) Distribute sheets of paper on which the follow-ing questions are printed. Ask all staff members to answer the questions from their perspective, according to their own beliefs about the correct answer, not as they think you want them to or as the practice now exists (unless the question specifically asks that). Here are the questions:

+ What business are we in?

+ Why are we in this business?

+ Who are our customers? (Remind them that more than one answer is possible.)

+ Who should our customers be?

+ What are our customers' expectations?

+ What image do we want (what do we want our customers to think of when they think of us)?

+ What should we be doing and saying to meet our customers' expectations and to reinforce our desired image?

Veterinarians and employees alike are likely to find this exercise and the ensuing discussion extremely interest-ing and enlightening. Depending on your employees, how well you've educated them about your practice and values, how well and how often you reinforce this message, and the length of time they've been with you, you may discover that their answers are similar to yours.

How To Brainstorm Effectively

Brainstorming is a method of encouraging the free flow of creative ideas in a group setting. Because the group may inhibit creativity and imagination, the leader should present these guidelines:

1. Permit no criticism or negativity. There are no bad or dumb ideas.

2. Record ideas exactly as the individual states them.

3. Focus ideas on processes, not people.

4. Give the group several minutes for each question or topic to think about or jot down their ideas.

5. Prime the pump by offering a few ideas if needed.

6. For each issue or question, first solicit thoughts and ideas randomly. When spontaneous suggestions taper off, encourage ideas from any group member(s) who has not offered one. Some people are naturally shy or inhibited in this setting.

Or you may discover that a broad chasm separates your views and theirs.

If your staff members are hesitant to respond, the brainstorming technique may be helpful to get them thinking creatively. Sometimes a group situation can inhibit individual expression of new ideas or opinions; brainstorming can overcome this. It's important not to use this exercise as a punitive measure. No person's views should be held against him or her. The purpose of this discussion is to first brainstorm, then come to agreement: "We are in the business of keeping pets healthy," or "We are in the business of caring for pets and their owners," or whatever you decide your business is.

Gain a Consensus of Attitudes and Values

A *consensus* is an opinion or statement that reflects the majority of the group and can be supported by all. Although consensus is a majority opinion, it does not entail a show of hands or other vote counting.

Once you discuss and agree on what business you're in and who your customers are—clients, veterinarians, family members, each other, employers, members of the community—go through each of the remaining questions and come up with a set of reasonable responses that reflect consensus attitudes and beliefs.

You may have an outlier—a staff member whose views are divergent from those of the rest of the group. If his or her views are negative (for example, if he or she holds a dim view of clients and their expectations), you or a senior staff member must work closely with this person in the future to encourage participation. After extensive discussion, if this individual cannot, or chooses not to, share the consensus perspective, you probably should suggest that he or she look elsewhere for an employer with a more similar outlook.

Developing a Mission Statement

After completing the previous activities, you will have the basis for developing a *mission statement*. Your mission statement can be specific and extensive, or broader and succinct. A mission statement clearly defines and determines decisions and behavior.

Let's look at developing a mission statement from the perspective of a small-animal practice with a special interest in avian medicine.

✦ *What business are we in?*

Helping pet owners keep their dogs, cats, and birds healthy.

✦ *Why are we in this business?*

To satisfy a personal need to help animals and people, and to make a reasonable profit for the practice.

✦ *Who are our customers?*

People who keep dogs, cats, and birds as pets; breeders; other veterinarians, especially those who don't work with birds; and each other.

✦ *Who should our customers be?*

All of the above.

✦ *What are the expectations of our customers?*

To have their needs, as they define or perceive them, met.

✦ *What image do we want (what do we want our customers to think of when they think of us)?*

A practice made up of compassionate, skilled professionals who have the most current technical knowledge and who go out of their way to satisfy clients. We want not only to provide the highest quality of clinical care but also to give our customers *more* than they want, need, or expect whenever we can.

✦ *What should we be doing and saying to meet our customers' expectations and to reinforce our desired image?*

We must unify our words and actions toward our clients, referral sources, and each other. We must always try to look at our practice, our actions, and our words through the eyes and ears of our customers.

On the basis of this discussion, the following statement could be created:

> *Our mission is to help our clients keep their pets healthy by providing superior preventive medicine, diagnosis, and treatment of disease, and personal attention. We will listen to our clients and communicate with them about their pets' condition and treatment, and we will treat them with the dignity, compassion, and courtesy we would expect for ourselves. We will treat our coworkers and colleagues as friends and professionals in the process of serving our clients. We will always strive to enjoy what we do.*

Figure 5.1 shows the mission statement developed by The Veterinary Medical Group of Des Moines. Compare it with the mission statement in Figure 5.2 of the Highland Hospital for Animals, and use the two statements to stimulate discussion and ideas for developing a mission statement for your own practice.

Figure 5.1 The Veterinary Medical Group of Des Moines

OUR MISSION

We are dedicated and determined patient advocates, anchored by our acknowledgment that to be an animal care-giver is a "calling." We are committed to maintaining and improving the quality of life of our animal patients by encouraging client and employee education, perpetuating American Animal Hospital Association principles and standards, and providing the highest quality medicine, surgery, and services possible through our equipment and facilities.

Provided courtesy of Dr. Marv Johnson, Director, The Veterinary Medical Group of Des Moines, IA

Figure 5.2 Highland Hospital for Animals

MISSION STATEMENT

It is our privilege to be caregivers to those pets and family members entrusted to our care by some very special people... our clients.
To that end, we will encourage each other with mutual support, inspiration, and vision of common goals. We will grow together to meet the ever-changing needs of our clients and their pets with knowledge, efficiency, and compassion. Our efforts must also enable us to meet the financial needs of the hospital and staff. Our profitability should enable all current hospital and staff expenses to be met as well as allow for future planning and growth. What is gained by all will be shared by all.

PRACTICE OBJECTIVES

My vision for Highland Hospital for Animals is to create an environment where these four objectives can be met:
1. Our patients receive the very best medical and surgical care we can offer with the personnel, expertise and equipment we have available.

2. Our clients receive respect, understanding, compassion and efficiency.

3. Individual staff members are challenged and supported by each other to grow personally and professionally.

4. The human-animal bond is recognized, celebrated, and promoted.

Provided courtesy of Dr. Greg Ekdale, owner of the Highland Hospital for Animals, Bloomington, IL

Dr. Greg Ekdale says of Highland Hospital for Animals' statement:

> Our mission statement was produced by our entire staff during regular staff meetings over a four- to six-month period several years ago. Recently we started a semi-annual series of presentations by our veterinarians and practice manager to our staff, which we call the 'Vision series.' The intent of these presentations is to let the staff know where our priorities lie and where emphasis will be placed in the months ahead. These three- to four-hour meetings are held away from the practice in a relaxed setting. We have held three Vision meetings so far. To date they have been well received by our staff.

When you've created a mission statement, don't file it away in a manila folder. Use it. Live it. Print it on the back of your business card. Frame it and hang it in the reception area where staff and clients can see it (and hold you to it). If it's brief, consider putting it on the bottom of your letterhead. Include it in your practice brochure, policy manual, and employee handbook. Have new employees sign a copy as a personal quality pledge.

Defining Objectives and Standards

A mission statement serves as the foundation for *practice objectives* and *service standards*, which form a more specific expression of what you intend to accomplish. This helps to remove uncertainties about the focus of the practice or your intended purpose. Whereas the *mission statement* says, "This is what we are about," the *objectives* say, "Here's how we intend to go about it." Objectives are goals: specific, achievable, and measurable, and preferably with a timeframe or date attached, as well as a description of who is responsible for carrying out the objectives. To be effective, objectives should "stretch" the practice and get employees *and* veterinarians out of "in-a-rut" thinking and behaving. Figure 5.2 includes objectives for the Highland Hospital for Animals.

Action Steps for Creating a Vision

1. Embrace your role as leader.

2. Define your own mission: Examine your beliefs, attitudes, and core values regarding the purpose of your practice, the role of your staff, and your personal and professional style.

3. Through discussion, develop a unified understanding of the business you're in, your customers, their expectations, and your current and desired image.

4. Seek staff input; use brainstorming to encourage staff to share ideas fully.

5. Together, use the responses to the questions and discussions to frame a mission statement in which everyone believes and that is realistic, optimistic, and achievable.

6. Make your mission statement highly visible in your practice.

7. Use your mission statement to define practice objectives and service standards that require continual stretching.

Defining objectives and standards is far from easy. It takes time, commitment, and planning, just as developing a mission statement does. We'll show you how to begin defining service standards in the next chapter.

Notes

1. J. A. Barker. *Future Edge*. New York: Wm. Morrow & Co., 1992: 163.
2. Rose. Now Quality Means Service Too. *Fortune*, April 22, 1992: 99–108.
3. J. Ballard. Lexington Boulevard Animal Hospital. *AAHA Trends*, Jun/Jul 1990: 20–21.

Chapter 6

Standards: Minimum Requirements for Maximum Service

I didn't know that's how I was supposed to do it!

Chris calls clients only if there's an abnormal lab test, so I figured that sounded good enough to me.

Do statements like these have a familiar ring? Do employees in your practice follow precedent or habit, right or wrong, because no guidelines or standards are in place prescribing minimum requirements or objectives? Does everyone have his or her own standards for everything from how long a client should wait to have a phone call returned to how veterinary records are completed?

Would you accept imprecise language or variability in treating your patients? Hardly. You adhere to standards for everything from blood glucose levels for diagnosing diabetes to millimeters of tears produced in a Schirmer tear test, for diagnosing keratoconjunctivitis sicca.

In the nonclinical activities of a veterinary practice, standards eliminate variation in activities and results, reduce confusion, clarify expectations, and simplify routine decision making. Standards help ensure reliable methods—precise, consistent, explicit, and tested ways of achieving a sought-after outcome. They also serve as a base for measuring quality of performance and service. Areas in which standards may be applied in a practice include appearance of the clinic, organization of the patient chart, telephone answering procedures, waiting time, and follow-up for complaints. You might want to model your own chart on the one in Table 6.1.

Standards make decision making easier and reduce the likelihood of errors. Setting standards frees you and your staff to concentrate on significant activities, because each standard removes uncertainty ("Mrs. Brooks has been waiting for thirty minutes in the exam room. I wonder if I should tell Dr. Egan he's running behind?") and makes the appropriate action clear ("Mrs. Brooks has been waiting for almost ten minutes. I'll tell her the doctor is running a little behind and ask if she would like a cup of tea, and I'll tell Dr. Egan that she's been waiting.")

Standards provide veterinarian(s) and their staffs with personal and collective goals. Unlike goals, however, standards should be immediately and consistently achievable. Goals, in contrast, are targets to aim for, with the expectation that they may not be realized immediately.

Standards to Please Veterinarian, Staff, *and* Clients

"I'm usually scared to call my vet's office because the assistants are rude and unfriendly," says a cat owner. "Everyone in my town agrees, but the vets are really good, and they never charge office call fees. If you take your cat in and it gets a clean bill of health, they won't charge you."

This woman's veterinarian has decided that his clients' priority is receiving a free office visit. He assumes they don't (and can't) understand that time and skills are required to determine whether a pet is healthy. Perhaps if he were to charge for every exam, he could afford to hire and train good staff members to provide friendly, helpful client service. (The problem here may not be

Table 6.1 Charting Standards for Client Experiences

Client Expectation	Office Standard
Phone answered promptly	Phone answered within three rings with a smile, using name and practice name.
Arrival acknowledged	Client greeted by name within 30 seconds of arrival.
Brief wait in reception area	Wait of no longer than 10 minutes beyond scheduled appointment time; client informed of any delays.
Friendly, helpful staff	Staff members educated and trained to answer typical questions. Staff addresses people and pets by name.
Friendly, knowledgeable doctor	Doctor spends at least 15 minutes with each client, actively listens to client concerns, and explains all procedures. Before they leave, all clients are asked, "Do you have any other questions or concerns?"
Clear take-home instructions for medication	Staff member shows client how to administer medication before it is dispensed. Verbal and written information about medication's use, indications, and side effects are given.
Staff members look professional	Staff members wear designated uniforms and name tags.

inherently rude staff members but, instead, overworked people with inadequate training.)

Veterinarians and staff should determine jointly what appropriate standards should be, using client wishes or expectations as a gauge. Assuming that you know what your clients want is risky. The standards for your practice should be designed to meet your clients' needs.

The techniques described in Chapter 3 for ascertaining client expectations will help you determine what your standards should be.

Developing Standards and Protocols for Service

Just as the highest-quality clinical care occurs when *medical* standards are adhered to, developing and following *service* standards in your practice will help you achieve or surpass client expectations (see Table 6.1). Developing service standards is a group effort. Veterinarians should bring together the practice staff or department staff and focus on only one service process at a time, for example, client check-in. Expectations are to be discussed at each step in the process and a protocol established for behaviors or a numerical standard that at minimum meets the expectation. Expected behaviors should be described as clearly and specifically as possible. For example, rather than, "Client will be greeted in a friendly manner," the standard would specify, "Client will be greeted by name—using Mr., Mrs., Ms., or Miss and the last name—with a smile, within ten seconds." This indicates clearly that the behavior is to be professional, friendly, and courteous.

These "soft" standards are important determinants of client satisfaction. Evidence shows that client satisfaction is significantly higher when friendliness accompanies competence.

In setting standards, processes are dissected as a series of activities. Each step of the activity or encounter is broken down to determine the individual events that create the final outcome.

This process is repeated for every service encounter your clients have. Your standards are incorporated into written job descriptions (see Chapter 8). You may wish to do this activity over a period of many weeks or months, depending on the size of your practice and the current level of client satisfaction.

Paying Attention to Detail

Staff members should be encouraged to come up with ways to exceed expectations either via the standard or through an unexpected "value-added" process or product. Value-added behaviors are those that will surprise clients and exceed their expectations. For example, the client's expectation upon signing in may simply be that he or she will be acknowledged within a reasonable time. If the receptionist looks up within 30 seconds of the client's arrival, smiles, and says, "Hi, please have a seat," the client's expectation is met. But if the receptionist smiles warmly and says, "Hello, Ms. Chang, it's nice to see you! You're here to see Dr. Milos today, aren't you? May I get you some coffee or juice?" the client is pleasantly surprised and pleased.

In addition to documenting the steps of the process, the customer and the owner of each activity must be acknowledged. (By owner, we're referring to a veterinarian or staff member ultimately responsible for the activity.) In specifying the customer and the owner, understanding dawns that *the customer at certain points in the process may be a fellow employee* rather than the client. Practices and veterinarians have internal as well as external customers.

This systematic process of delineating activities, behaviors, and expectations, and then setting appropriate standards, brings reliability and predictability to the practice. It allows greater flexibility and productivity. Staff energies are focused on client care and client satisfaction issues rather than on repairing mistakes and apologizing for problems that could have been prevented.

Setting an Example

Veterinarians set an example by adhering to standards themselves. If staff members notice that the doctor doesn't adhere to standards, why should they?

In setting standards in a practice that has not followed them previously, all members have to be committed to and comply with the standards. Otherwise you may experience a situation such as this one, described by a relief veterinarian:

> I was hired to work the same week that the hospital had hired a new receptionist. I had worked in this hospital before and knew they had a phone policy. I could see that the receptionist was trying to carry out the policy as described, but the technician kept

interrupting her to ask minor questions or even to correct what she was saying while she was still on the phone! That certainly didn't convey a good impression to the clients.

New employees usually are the least empowered because they have no seniority, power base, support group, or credibility. Veterinarians should rely on the people who have been there the longest and get their commitment in helping to develop and maintain the standards.

Setting Internal Standards

Standards shouldn't be limited to client interactions. The staff needs guidelines for routine hospital tasks, too. How often should the bathroom be cleaned, and who is to be in charge of that task? Who makes sure that no cobwebs are forming in the corners of the exam rooms?

Dr. April Marklin created detailed daily and weekly task lists to get around the typical staff complaints of *"she* always looks busy, but *I'm* doing all the work!" Employees initial each task as it is completed.

> *The charts allow us to monitor work performance without having to actually watch the employees perform each duty. The most significant reward we've seen has been the change in attitudes. Now everyone works as a team.*[1]

Dr. Marklin's daily list was divided into morning and evening chores and covered pet feeding, sweeping, loading and unloading the dishwasher, and doing the wash. Her weekly list included vacuuming the doctor's office, cleaning the vents in all the rooms, and dusting pictures in the waiting room. Consider involving your staff in making up lists for *your* practice.

Risks and Benefits of Standards

A follow-up action can determine how you're doing and whether you need to reassess client expectations and practice protocols. Are your standards realistic and achievable? If not, what is standing in your way, and how can you remove those hurdles?

Action Steps for Setting Standards

1. Bring staff members together to analyze areas and activities in the practice to which standards should be applied.

2. Set standards according to client expectations and needs, not merely for the convenience of veterinarians or staff.

3. Review standards with all employees, new and old, to ensure consistency of attitude and actions.

4. Set standards not only for areas and activities that clients see but also for internal processes: paperwork, staff-to-staff behavior, and the like. Internal customers are as important as external customers.

5. Review practice standards regularly to determine whether they should be modified or raised. As service quality improves, client expectations will increase.

Standards provide continuity and consistency, evidence of quality, and a level of comfort to veterinarians, staff, and clients alike. Standards also entail risk. When practice standards are monitored, any deviation is glaring. Clients become acclimated to service excellence; eventually it becomes their expectation. If your schedule runs smoothly and efficiently 99% of the time and clients are escorted to the exam room within 10 minutes, this becomes the expected standard. Clients will overlook an occasional knot in the schedule that causes them to wait (although they're more likely to be forgiving if an explanation and apology accompany the error). If waiting time lengthens to 20 minutes on several occasions, however, clients are likely to become suspicious and skeptical. They have learned not to expect this. Setting standards escalates expectations. Failure to achieve the standards increases customer disappointment.

The benefits to a practice that establishes, follows, and improves standards are many. For veterinarians, benefits are found in fewer recurring problems and questions and the improved productivity that efficiency brings. For staff, benefits consist of the continuity, freedom, and diminished uncertainty that documented requirements provide. Clients gain the pleasure of a predictable and positive experience. All members of the practice team—veterinarians, clients, and staff—enjoy an atmosphere of pride, pleasure, and accomplishment.

Notes

1. A. Marklin. A Chart-busting Idea for the Staff Turned the Practice Around! *Veterinary Economics*, Sept 1995: 90-91.

Chapter 7

Staff Satisfaction and Teamwork

Q: How do you get people to do what you want them to?

A: You don't. People do what they want, not what you want.

Your task is to get your team members to want the same things you do: to aim for the same goals—quality service and satisfied clients—and to seek the success you want in your practice. Getting people to work willingly toward a common objective is what motivation is all about.

Getting People To Do What You Want

How do you get your staff to do what you want? How do you motivate your staff members? If money is the primary motivator in your practice, you are probably wondering why your employees don't stay or don't care or why they're always angling for bigger raises or better bonuses.

People do work for money—it's an extrinsic reward for their effort—but they also work for intrinsic rewards such as recognition and personal satisfaction. Money becomes important as a motivator when salaries are at the low end of the wage scale or not competitive with those of similar jobs in the marketplace.

Figure 7.1 What Motivates Employees?

✔ Appreciation for work performed

✔ Participation in workplace information and decisions

✔ Understanding attitude by supervisor

✔ Job security

✔ Good wages

✔ Interesting work

✔ Promotion opportunities

✔ Loyalty from management

✔ Good working conditions

✔ Tactful discipline

You may recall learning in Psychology 101 class about Maslow's hierarchy of needs. According to Maslow's hierarchy of needs, once a person's basic physical needs (food, air, shelter, and safety) are met, the social needs (belonging, esteem, and recognition) become more important. If you meet your staff's basic needs with competitive salaries, good benefits, and a pleasant work environment, you'll find that intrinsic rewards are powerful motivators.

Figure 7.1 presents a list of motivators. You are to rank them in order according to what you think your staff respond to most. Then give the same list to your employees and ask each person to rank the items in order of what's most important to him or her. The results of this exercise can serve as an excellent discussion topic for staff meetings. It is also a good means of determining what motivates individual employees.

A few people are self-motivated; they have an internal drive that propels them to do their best no matter what's going on around them. But the dilemma facing many practice managers and veterinarians is this: What works most consistently to keep people motivated? The broad answer is recognition, appreciation, and participation. Many veterinary hospital employees rate an interesting job, appreciation for a job well done, and open communication higher on their list of needs than an increase in pay.[1]

The detailed answer is that each of these motivators works for someone, sometime. Usually a mix of motivators—some financial, some verbal, and some tangible—is what keeps people excited and enthusiastic about continually stretching to reach the target. No reward will work, however, unless it is tied to personal and practice goals and service standards. People need to know what success looks like, what the reward is for. For example, if client satisfaction is the goal of the practice, individual and team rewards should be related to staff participation in measurable client satisfaction results.

Inspiring Your Team

Before setting up individual rewards, take a look at the overall atmosphere in your practice. The following organizational characteristics must be present for people to become and remain motivated to work toward practice goals:

✦ *Participation.* Involve the staff in decision making, goal setting, planning, and problem solving whenever possible. People own what they create. If staff members feel a sense of ownership and participation in the practice, they will be motivated to improve their skills and service continually because they realize that success of the practice reflects on them.

✦ *Values.* Make the philosophy of client-centered service known through your actions and words. Continually reinforce the values and philosophy of the practice through public recognition of actions that exemplify it and constructive, private correction of actions that diminish it.

✦ *Personal power.* Organizations large and small are discovering that giving people the authority to make decisions on their own makes them more productive and more committed; their morale improves as well (Chapter 8 addresses empowerment in more depth).

✦ *Challenge.* Provide challenging work, and encourage career development through information, added responsibilities, and training.

✦ *Communication.* Keep communication flowing up, down, and across all lines and levels in the practice. Use formal communication methods—staff meetings, memos, newsletters, and one-on-one discussions—as well as informal methods. You don't have to have heart-to-heart chats with every staff member. Your practice manager or team leader should listen and respond to specific staff concerns. Staff members should strive to understand the organization's mission and their importance as individuals and team members in helping achieve quality service.

Making Staff Meetings Fun and Useful

Nothing is worse than a meeting held just to hold a meeting. Don't let prior experience with useless meetings turn you off to the whole idea of meetings, though. The communication that results from regular meetings helps foster teamwork. The most effective practices with the most active teams hold regular staff meetings no matter how busy they are.

Schedule regular staff meetings, and assign different team members to run them. Sometimes people are fearful to make decisions even though they are given the right to. It may require some tactful coaching (provide sample agendas, for example).

Consider holding "stand-up meetings" to start the day. Everybody participates, and the purpose is to share the day's scheduled activities. ("Dr. A. will be in surgery all day, Dr. B. is at a conference, and Dr. C. will be here. The front office is swamped because Marjie is out sick— let's call and tell her hi, maybe send flowers—and there's a new kennel assistant starting today—welcome! Does anybody have a special project or need help today? Let's all stay in close touch with the workload of the front office staff. If there's a way we can help while you're short-staffed, let us know.")

Group practices with large staffs could follow the example of Dr. Thomas Austin of the six-veterinarian Newport Harbor Animal Hospital in Costa Mesa, CA. He says, "It's not common for us to have our entire staff together, but we do a lot of work in teams. Each team has its own separate meeting."

Is finding the time for staff meetings a problem? Try this method. It lasts 10 to 20 minutes maximum and is held every 2 to 4 weeks—in every department for a large practice or practicewide for a small practice. Make a commitment to hold these meetings at specific intervals. The purpose of the meeting is to resolve problems, build morale, establish trust, quell rumors, and generate ideas—in short, to communicate.

Led by a strong facilitator, the meeting consists of brief statements of needs, information, problem situations, and questions. Each statement or question is followed by a desired action, agreement about the person(s) responsible for the action, and an assigned completion or follow-up date. Minutes are kept and reviewed quickly at the end of the meeting to verify group consensus on the statements, actions, and responsibilities. A copy of the minutes goes to each individual responsible for action. It's an effective approach for a practice that claims, "We don't have time for meetings."

Hiring Attitude, Not Just Skills

Getting people to participate and stay motivated is much easier if they have a positive outlook from the start. Many hiring experts agree that successful hiring is a result of emphasis on attitude, not simply skills. They recommend that you *hire for attitude and train for performance*. After all, you can teach employees how to perform a urinalysis, but you can't teach them how to care about the practice and your clients. Do what the major leaguers do to create a great team: Scout potential players carefully, and always call their references.

Thorough, in-depth interviews of potential candidates can reveal much about a person's attitude, values, and work ethic. Not everyone wants autonomy, challenge, and responsibility. Through skillful interviewing of job applicants, you can avoid bringing these people into your practice.

Don't skimp on quality people. When your practice becomes known as a great place to work because you offer a higher salary, better benefits, and a pleasant work environment, you can select from the best staff candidates available.

What's more, motivated and satisfied staff members become long-term members of your team, reducing turnover. As a Georgia pet owner says of her veterinarian's practice, "It's impressive that there's such a low turnover. I think it means that it must be a good place to work."[2] You can see the cost of turnover in your practice: the direct costs of advertising to fill vacant positions, severance pay, and similar expenses. You don't even want to calculate the indirect costs: lost productivity as a result of vacancies and the need to yank an experienced staffer from her job to train the new person, and the impact of poor morale on productivity and efficiency.

Making Employees Feel Safe

Keeping staff members satisfied requires creating a safe workplace—safe from injury, accidents, and hazards unique to veterinary medicine. Like many veterinarians, you may see OSHA as a group formed to give you a headache. Although that may be the result, the intention is to create a safe workplace for your employees. Complying with OSHA standards shows that you are committed to the well-being of all your staff members. It also helps to reduce the number of worker's compensation claims (as well as liability; a major cause of client lawsuits is slips and falls).

Sometimes special situations require special consideration. Whether your technician's allergy to formaldehyde prevents him from assisting with certain lab procedures, or another technician's pregnancy requires her to avoid radiation, cross-training your staff will demonstrate that attention to safety doesn't mean your business has to run any less smoothly. (Cross-training has loads of other benefits, too. More about that in the next chapter.)

Create a safety education program for your practice. Such programs include training new staff members about problems unique to veterinary practice, avoiding injuries, and appropriate responses to accidents.

Speaking of safe, do your employees feel safe from sexual harassment? In this area more than any other, employees must feel that they can voice their concerns without retribution. An effective sexual harassment policy should include specific guidelines about how a complaint is registered and to whom, and the procedure for evaluating and following through on each complaint. It should include several options of where employees can turn for help, as a problem with one of the "bosses" cannot be brought to the boss's attention. The AVMA *Membership Directory and Resource Manual* includes a model policy on harassment.

Keeping the Staff Motivated

Let's say you're doing everything we've discussed. You hire people with a great attitude, you have regular staff meetings, you've created a safe workplace, you offer plenty of opportunities for learning and growth, and staff members solve problems independently every day.

How do you keep employees motivated, excited about their work, interested in providing the highest level of service, and constantly looking for ways to do things better? How do you get them to strive for top-quality service and satisfied clients as much as you do?

First you make it clear what the goal is, what the values of the practice are. You give employees information about the practice. You educate them and encourage them to seek education (knowledge is power in more ways than one). You give people tasks that allow them to exhibit responsibility, put them in control, and allow them to grow. When you see employees demonstrating the values and doing things that move them, and the practice, toward the goals, encourage, recognize, and reward them. Although the reward will depend on the situation and the individual, some assumptions can be made about workplace motivators. Management expert Frederick Herzberg says the factors that contribute to job satisfaction fall into the following categories[3]:

+ achievement

+ recognition

+ the work itself

+ responsibility

+ advancement

+ growth

Herzberg also suggests that certain factors contribute greatly to job dissatisfaction. Characterized as "hygiene" factors, they include company policy, supervision, work conditions, salary, relationship with peers and subordinates, personal life, status, and security.

If you want your staff to be satisfied with their jobs and motivated to perform, concentrate on enhancing the motivators—achievement, recognition, responsibility, advancement, and growth—and diminishing the impact of the "dissatisfiers"—the rules and regulations, unpleasant working conditions, and supervisor-employee stress.[4]

To keep employees motivated, enrich their jobs. Job enrichment means making work meaningful. Rather than simplifying the receptionist's tasks, add responsibility, such as the reception area refreshment cart. This means the receptionist is completely responsible for this task, including selecting, ordering, and maintaining the refreshments in addition to offering them to waiting clients. Herzberg calls this "vertical job loading."

Recognizing and Rewarding the Staff

Veterinarians and practice managers in practices with "enriched" jobs contend that recognition and rewards also play a role in motivation. We agree. As Michael LeBouef said in *How To Win Customers and Keep Them for Life*, "You get more of the behavior you reward. You don't get what you hope for, ask for, wish for, or beg for. You get what you reward."[5]

What forms of recognition and rewards work best for your team? We suggest that you choose the motivators that best fit the needs of your practice and your employees. Consider the following.

Competitive Salaries

Are your salaries competitive? Offering wages that are slightly higher than normal allows you to "skim the cream," to choose the absolute best from the job pool. It also ensures that the needs on the bottom tier of Maslow's hierarchy are satisfied so you can concentrate on the social motivators. Equally important, wages say a great deal about how much you value the responsibilities of a job. For example, if the philosophy in your practice is quality service and quality care but your receptionist is paid minimum wages, your message is clear: "We don't really mean it!"

Dr. Austin points out, "Employees have to feel like they have a sense of ownership. They aren't motivated by money, but they can be demotivated if their salary doesn't fit with their efforts."

Appropriate Benefits

Does your benefits package really provide what employees want? Could you offer personal days off in some reasonable ratio to unused sick time? Would a "cafeteria plan" of benefits meet a greater variety of employee needs? How do you handle pet-care benefits for your employees? If a major benefit is discounts on pet health care, an employee with only a few pets may feel a sense of injustice if another employee has several pets and overutilizes that benefit. Potential inequities can be mitigated by providing choices and setting limits.

Sharing Profits

Last, and equally important, is the benefit of sharing profits. Even if money itself is not a primary motivator for employees, the ownership that profit sharing conveys often is. If your employees have a stake in the success of the practice, they will show a zeal for efficiency and profitability. This accountability will translate into personal satisfaction when they see the results from their efforts.

Financial incentive programs encourage and reward achievement of practice goals. Goals to strive for include reduction in accounts receivable, a monthly or quarterly revenue target, and scheduling of new client appointments or dentistries. If something is important to the practice, make it important to the staff, and reward employees for their part in reaching the goal. (If you set targets and don't reach them, don't chastise; bring the staff together to review the goal and to analyze how it can be reached.) Incentive rewards should be distributed frequently enough to motivate (at least quarterly or, better yet, monthly).

A system used in some practices is to dedicate a portion of the revenue from the practice to a staff incentive pool. Every 6 months the account is reconciled with actual expenses. Employees receive a bonus if staff salary expenses are lower than that percentage of revenues. This encourages efforts toward client satisfaction (which encourages referrals) and a strong desire for efficiency.

Consistent and Frequent Rewards

Your staff's "culture" will determine much of what's right for your employees (see Figure 7.2 for ideas). Some practices are run like a big family, and others take a more businesslike approach. The atmosphere in your practice will depend on how you and your colleagues view yourself and your employees as well as the size and type of practice. Regardless of the culture in your practice, reward your employees with a fair, consistent hand, and do it frequently. Show no favoritism, and be clear about what you're doing: You're saying "thank you" for a job well done.

How will you know when it's appropriate to reward? The key is that everyone knows what's expected. Do you have written practice standards and job descriptions? Do you give regular performance appraisals? (see Chapter 8). Only when you define what's expected can you and your staff members know when those expectations have been exceeded.

The rewards *you* earn for motivating your staff with recognition and rewards? There are many: Lower worker's compensation costs, greater retention, easier recruitment, higher morale, greater trust, improved productivity, and better service to customers.[5]

Making People Feel Important

Remember this principle: *Please make me feel important.* People want to feel valued, a part of the team. Seek a balance between recognizing and rewarding team accomplishments and individual accomplishments. Everyone wants to be a part of a group—a team—but each person also wants acknowledgment for his or her individual uniqueness. Honor your team's outstanding effort, but also honor contributions by members who deserve it.

Figure 7.2 Staff Recognition and Rewards

Incentives That Motivate

✦ Letter of thanks or appreciation mailed to employee's home, copy in personnel file and copy on bulletin board

✦ Immediate, sincere, verbal compliment or recognition from veterinarian

✦ Business cards for every staff member

Instant Rewards

✦ Flowers or green plant

✦ Books

✦ Gift certificates

✦ Goofy gifts

✦ $1 or $5 bill handed out to show appreciation spontaneously

✦ Certificates ("Thank You-Grams," "You Did It" award)

Success Celebrations

✦ Lunch or dinner gift certificate for employee and spouse

✦ Department store shopping spree

✦ Half-day off with pay

✦ Ice cream social or pot luck

Team Incentives

✦ Regular staff meetings

✦ Close practice for educational seminar

✦ Lunch paid for by the practice

✦ Parties and special events

✦ Open house planned by staff

✦ Strategic planning session or staff retreat

✦ Educational opportunities paid for by the practice

Financial Rewards

✦ Salary and benefits increases

✦ Reduced work-week hours (with the same salary)

✦ Interim bonuses for specific outstanding achievement (e.g., $25)

✦ Bonus plan tied to specific (employee or practice) goals

It's important for the veterinarian(s) to acknowledge good work, perhaps even more important than for the practice manager or team leader to do so. It may be difficult for you and your practice partners to catch staff in the act of doing good, so you must make an effort to be observant. Look for little things—the receptionist assisting an elderly client to a seat in the reception area—and also ask your manager to inform you of acts that deserve recognition.

Share customer compliments about the practice and/or individual employees with the person mentioned and the whole staff. Post letters of praise in a central place, and put a copy in the employee's personnel file. Send a copy to the employee's home, along with your own note of thanks, so that the individual can share the glory with family members.

Create a special award to recognize outstanding employees. Watch for actions that show an employee's commitment to and understanding of the practice philosophy. Ask managers and supervisors to let you know when an employee should be recognized. Use bonuses to reward achievement of practice goals and personal job-related achievements. Some practices name an Employee of the Month or similar outstanding staffer. Although official recognitions are important, be careful about setting a precedent for a regular award, especially if you have a small staff. You'll soon be faced with the dilemma of what to do when one employee keeps winning the award, to the detriment of the rest of the staff's morale. It's usually better to make awards official but to only give them out for specific situations. When you see an opportunity to recognize an achievement, do it.

Buy gift certificates for manicures, a round of golf, a dinner for two, an afternoon at the zoo, or an evening at the movies. Keep them on hand and present them to employees when they need or deserve a little boost.

Recognizing Unique Contributions

Reward all kinds of contributions. In *Team Players and Teamwork: The New Competitive Business Strategy*, author Glenn Parker describes four types of players on a team: contributors, collaborators, communicators, and challengers.[7] Each is an equally important team member with unique personality traits. Understanding these types can enhance team productivity and build consensus. These ideas, the Myers-Briggs test (a personality type indicator), and books will help you understand different personalities and how they contribute to your workplace.[8,9]

A veterinarian in the Southwest recalls this about her former job:

> Everyone in our clinic read a book about personality profiles. I was able to see that my difficulty with getting to work absolutely on time (typically 5 to 6 minutes late) was in part due to certain personality traits. The problem was compounded by the fact that the boss's personality placed punctuality very high on his list of necessary traits in an employee.
>
> Another employee had the same problem. Our arriving a few minutes late nearly every day precipitated a bad mood in the boss, and the effects radiated all morning long. After identifying this, we made an extra effort to arrive on time, while the boss tried to understand our difficulty and to react less.
>
> One receptionist had a clear insight into and extreme empathy for client feelings. She was in charge of writing sympathy cards to clients who had lost pets and was able to help them through these times with follow-up phone calls. Technicians who had better animal skills ended up drifting to the back where they had fewer client interactions. If this kind of assessment were to be done early in employment, [employees] could be placed in the best situation for them rather than the usual drifting around, failing at several positions before finding the ideal situation.

One caveat: Personality tests are fun and can be helpful but should never be used as a means of making decisions about hiring, firing, or performance evaluation. Their use should not be required but, rather, suggested in an atmosphere of learning and sharing.

Fostering Team Spirit

Quality staff members feel proud to be part of your team, and teamwork is one of the most significant factors in ensuring quality service to your clients, day in and day out. Working together, the members of a team get things done efficiently and effectively, conveying confidence and competence to your clients.

To foster team spirit, take time for fun. Close your practice one afternoon a month for staff meetings and motivational talks, or just for fun. Buy lunch. Some veterinarians do it every day, making it part of the staff's benefits. The staff also is paid for these mandatory meetings because they are working through lunch.

Host socializing activities for you and your staff. Include families in some, and reserve some for staff only. Because families and individuals vary in how comfortable they are with after-hours activities, you have to be sensitive to your entire staff when planning outings. Make social activities optional to avoid liabilities that are incurred when you require employees to participate in more than their job responsibilities. Some veterinarians ban business talk during the event to promote camaraderie.

Throw a spontaneous celebration occasionally. Recognize the significance of small wins; they line the path leading to the big ones. One veterinarian keeps a bottle of sparkling cider in the refrigerator and opens it to celebrate when a particularly difficult case improves. When the staff stays late without complaint on a particularly frenetic day, order a basket of fresh muffins to greet them the next morning, along with a note that says simply, "Thanks for yesterday—and for coming back this morning!"

When employees are ill, call and check on them personally. Avoid sounding as if you're calling to see if they're really sick. Show your concern, and see whether they need anything.

Look around the technicians' station and lounge. Can you do anything to make their workplace more pleasant? You might buy a stereo system, a microwave oven, a coffee pot, a popcorn popper, or a lounge chair. Consult with them first, though. Whatever you do, affix to your gift a tasteful brass plate saying something like, "Thanks for all your hard work." This form of recognition makes the hospital staff, and you, feel good. It's a subtle, but wonderfully effective, form of marketing for your practice. Technicians and assistants can be superb referral sources for veterinarians and practices they respect.

Build fun into the workplace. Veterinarians, practice managers, and employees in busy practices say their focus is constantly "making our clients feel at home and happy with us." These veterinarians and staff work hard. They also take time to play. They incorporate games and humor into their staff meetings; they schedule bowling, comedy club, and other outings; and they celebrate birthdays.

Getting People Involved

If you think you're creating a great workplace for your employees, check with them to be sure that's the case. Consider passing around an employee survey to encourage specific comments. One, published in *Veterinary Economics*, asked employees how the practice met their needs in five areas: praise/recognition, economic security, emotional security, self-expression, and self-respect.[10]

According to Herzberg, the best form of motivation is the kind that gets people involved with what they do, making them feel that their efforts result in worthwhile contributions to the organization.[11] Does this sound a great deal like empowerment? It is. It's putting real responsibility on the individuals' shoulders and holding the individual accountable for what happens. It's giving them control. When people feel a sense of control, productivity soars and errors decline. In the next chapter we'll show you how.

Notes

1. M. Becker. DVM. Reward Your Champions. *Veterinary Economics*, Apr 1997: 92–95.
2. American Animal Hospital Association. *1995 AAHA Report: A Study of the Companion Animal Veterinary Services Market: 111*.
3. F. Herzberg. One More Time (How Do You Motivate Employees? *Harvard Business Review*, reprint no. 87507.
4. Herzberg.

Action Items for Staff Motivation and Teamwork

1. Hire quality people who demonstrate a service-oriented attitude.

2. Talk with each of your employees to understand what motivates each one to perform effectively.

3. Write accurate, realistic job descriptions based on the tasks that have to be accomplished in your practice.

4. Provide challenging work, and encourage career development.

5. Offer competitive salaries and benefits that meet your employees' needs.

6. Provide ongoing recognition, appreciation, and participation in decision making.

7. Keep communication flowing, formally and informally.

8. Empower your staff to make decisions and to contribute to the practice in meaningful ways.

9. Take time for fun!

5. M. LeBouef. *How To Win Customers and Keep Them for Life*. New York: Berkeley Publishing Group, 1987: 149.
6. L. R. Brecker. Circles Style Management Creates Committed Employees. *Advance for Physical Therapists*, July 6, 1992: 9–12.
7. G. M. Parker. *Team Players and Teamwork: The New Competitive Business Strategy*. San Francisco: Jossey-Bass Publishers, 1990:164.
8. M. Landsberg. *The Tao of Coaching: Boost Your Effectiveness by Inspiring Those Around You*. Santa Monica, CA: Knowledge Exchange, 1997: 43–50.
9. B. Bowers, Ph.D. *What Color Is Your Aura?* New York: Pocket Books/Simon and Schuster, 1989.
10. M. Becker, DVM. Celebrate Everyday Heroes. *Veterinary Economics*, June 1997:30–35.
11. Herzberg.

Chapter 8

Empowerment

It's not my job.

We don't do it that way here.

I'll have to ask . . . .

We've always done it this way!

The only thing worse than these lame, hollow excuses is the message they send to your clients and colleagues: You don't trust your employees' judgment (they aren't qualified for the job they're doing), they don't trust themselves to make good decisions, or they don't trust you to stand behind them when they do make a decision. These problems clog your practice with indecision and send a negative message to the world—and especially to your clients.

How can you change the negative to a positive, the "can't do it" to "can do it"? How do you create team members who not only are committed to client satisfaction but also have the knowledge and the authority to make sure it happens? You encourage independence and autonomy, also known as empowerment. Here's how:

✦ Hire people who welcome challenge and responsibility.

✦ Build confidence in your employees and your team by giving them information, ongoing educational opportunities, and organizational values and standards.

✦ Set forth clear expectations. A staff performs better when employees know what is expected of them.

✦ Train employees thoroughly, give them the resources they need, then hold them accountable for their areas of responsibilities and actions.

✦ Give your staff immediate and concrete feedback. The veterinarians, practice managers, and team leaders we interviewed follow this philosophy: Praise employees in public, and correct them in private. When they have made an error in judgment, chastise the action but not the individual. Then together come up with better options for similar situations in the future.

✦ Praise a job well done. When employees have made a good call, especially one involving some risk on their part, recognize their good work. Compliment exceptional actions liberally and frequently—verbally, in writing, and with occasional rewards such as bonuses or gifts. Ensure that good employees receive more praise than correction.

✦ Set limits so employees are comfortable making decisions within certain parameters. For instance, they may be authorized to take any necessary customer-pleasing or service recovery action with an expense limit up to $100. If a client is unhappy about the wait for a $35 visit, the front-office staff can waive the fee and alert the doctor so he or she can write a personal note apologizing for the inconvenience. If a piece of equipment breaks down and the repair or replacement is less than $100, they can get it fixed without delay.

✦ Treat your staff as a team, letting your clients and colleagues know you value your employees by the respect you show them. This gives their actions credibility in the eyes of others; they are viewed as acting on your behalf. The result is that your time is leveraged effectively and your "reach" is extended.

Creating a Wish List

Many practices hire good people but discourage and demoralize them quickly by asking them to do impossible tasks or poorly defined jobs or otherwise mismanaging them. Says one staffer, "I feel I'm not able to do my best job because I'm doing too many other temporary jobs for other people."[1]

Start by listing the tasks that need to be accomplished daily, weekly, monthly, and yearly. Make a list of the things that make the perfect practice. Do you want somebody answering the telephone for 12 hours a day, including lunch? Put it on the list. Do you want your clients called the day after discharge from the hospital? Put it on the list. Do you want your clients to receive their lab results within 24 hours if at all possible? Put it on the list. Do you want to collect 98% of your billings? Put it on the list. You get the idea. If it's important to you, write it down.

Now take a look at your list. How could you accomplish what's on it? Do you need two more front-office people instead of a technician? Would you be smarter to hire a technician, not another veterinarian, to ease your workload? Do you need a technician's assistant in addition to or rather than another technician? Do you need to change your work patterns?

Let your wish list define the skills or positions needed to help you accomplish it. When defining positions, list the personality traits required. For example, if yours is a particularly hectic front office and you'd like the atmosphere to be calmer, list "patient, cheerful, quiet, and calm" as attributes you value in that area. Next, define the job and the nuts and bolts of getting the job done. Be honest. Include the negatives as well as the positives. If there is a way to turn the negatives into positives, by all means, do it!

Providing Training

Once you find, interview, and hire the very best employees, provide thorough training. Too often, someone with potential is hired and tossed into a new environment with people he or she doesn't know, policies that are not spelled out, and rules that are never quite clear.

Make the new person feel welcome by assigning him or her a "buddy"—someone familiar with the practice, policies, and people—who can act as a mentor and get him or her off on the right foot. This will make and maintain a favorable impression of the practice in the new employee's mind.

An *employee policy manual* is helpful for letting staff know what's expected in terms of dress, professional behavior, confidentiality, and so forth. It doesn't have to be long and stuffy or crammed with legalese. Make the policies friendly but clear. In today's employment environment, in which discharging an employee can be difficult, the policy manual can serve as a framework for expectations. For help, consult AAHA's *Guide to Creating an Employee Handbook*.

Use a written checklist of orientation and training tasks to ensure that nothing is forgotten. Spend a few moments at the end of the day talking with new employees and emphasizing their importance in providing the best service your clients have ever encountered, no matter what department they work in. Ask them questions about where they feel competent, and when they feel lost, to discover where they need more help.

After your new employee is oriented, trained, and settled, what can you do if you discover you've made a mistake, that you've put a square peg into a round hole? Fix it fast. Don't wait for the problem to fix itself. It won't happen. If you're convinced that you have a winning employee in a poorly described or ill-matched job, change the job, the tasks, or the responsibilities.

If you've made a really big mistake, acknowledge it and terminate the relationship. Before you fire anybody, however, document the problems and use the job description to outline your expectations. Talk to the employee. Be sure that he or she has a chance to correct the problem. Many practices set up a 90-day probationary period for each new employee, clarifying that this is a time to get acquainted and to learn whether a longer relationship is advisable.

Providing Tactful Guidance

Specify expectations with written job descriptions (and occasionally ask employees how their actual work matches up with their job descriptions). What gets measured gets done. Every team member should have written standards and expectations for his or her position (see Chapter 6). Each employee should be evaluated at least annually, and preferably quarterly, to determine where he or she is meeting or exceeding expectations and where improvements are needed.

The best way to accomplish this is through a performance appraisal in which the employee has the opportunity to evaluate his or her own performance using the same form that the supervisor uses. During the performance evaluation compare the employee and supervisor appraisals. Develop written job-related goals with the employee for the coming 3-, 6-, or 12-month period. These goals should relate to the practice mission directly and indirectly. This gives both employee and supervisor specific measures of change and improvement. A sample performance appraisal can be found in Figure 8.1.

Even the most skilled, conscientious employees need guidance, coaching, and plenty of cheerleading along the way. Then they need to be let loose to do what you hired them to do: Give service, satisfy clients, and build a successful practice.

Some risks are inherent in empowering employees to do their jobs and a little more. What if they overreach? They will make mistakes occasionally. When they do, the mistake should be pointed out in private, along with the reason it is a mistake.

Recognizing that people do make mistakes, Dr. Richard Johnson, hospital director of the seven-veterinarian Broadway Animal Hospital in El Cajon, CA, turns each error into a positive learning experience.

> *I did my residency at the Animal Medical Center in New York, and the people I worked with there were not bashful about correcting one another immediately. Each time someone suggested a better way to do something, I learned from it. I have tried to apply that in my practice so that when I see a technician*

Figure 8.1 Performance Appraisal Form

Employee _____ Evaluator _____
Supervisor _____ Date of review _____
Date of hire _____ Date of last review _____
Performance scale: 0=poor; 1= below average; 2= average; 3= above average;
4= superior

Performance on the job: **Individual characteristics:**

Performance on the job		Individual characteristics	
Punctuality		Appearance	
Initiative	____	Service attitude	____
Dependability	____	Enthusiasm	____
Accuracy	____	Diplomacy	____
Ability to assume responsibility	____	Flexibility	____
Knowledge of procedures	____	Cooperation	____
Exercise of judgment	____	Verbal communication skills	____
Organizational skills	____	Written communication skills	____
Problem solving	____	Ability to follow directions	____
Pet interaction/handling	____	Interest in learning	____

Professional goals to be pursued in the next year: _____
_____
_____

Comments: _____
_____
_____

_____   _____
Employee's signature   Evaluator's signature

struggling with a procedure, I suggest a new approach. I expect my staff to correct me in the same manner.[2]

In *The Tao of Coaching* Max Landsberg describes three kinds of feedback: positive (praise), constructive (highlighting how the person could do better next time), and negative feedback (replaying what went wrong). Negative feedback is destructive, whereas positive and constructive feedback create trust and cooperation.[3]

Minimizing Your Risk

There's the risk that employees will do too much (managers fear that they'll give away the store). And there's also the risk that employees will draw the line too restrictively. The authors of *The Service Edge* tell of a bank in which line employees were given authority to make the check-cashing decisions traditionally reserved for branch management. The tellers wrote check-cashing regulations so restrictive that even the bank president had to show three forms of identification just to deposit his paycheck.[4] The problems here may have been a lack of thorough training of the tellers regarding the bank's customer service philosophy and an environment that was not threat-free.

Empowerment gives individuals (or teams) the ability and the authority to act in the best interests of the customer and the organization, particularly when unusual or unpredictable events or activities arise that require an immediate response. When you empower your staff, you give them autonomy. You credit them with intelligence. You permit and encourage them to act with some degree of independence in making decisions that may extend beyond the normal realm of their authority, as a team as well as individually.

Dr. Gary Johnson, one of two veterinarians at Dana Niguel Veterinary Hospital in Dana Point, CA, understands the benefits of empowerment.

> *Our receptionists have the liberty and authority to make things right. For instance, if a client has a complaint about charges, the receptionist can explain why a particular charge was made. She might remove it for that particular visit but explain that it would be charged in the future under the same circumstances.*

In empowered organizations, individuals and teams have the authority—even the requirement—to act when atypical events arise, sometimes taking action that goes beyond the boundaries of their usual restrictions and limitations. What scares many managers, and even some employees, is the fuzziness of autonomy, the fact that appropriate actions, responsibilities, authority, and limits are not always clear.[5]

Sometimes unusual events occur that don't fit into the routine tasks or individual limitations. To define and clarify the scope of acceptable actions, you must allow the employee to act when these events arise. It helps if you've discussed general guidelines ("Use your best judgment to solve problems;" "Write off a charge up to $___ under these circumstances"). How far and how quickly you extend an employee's authority depends on the judgment he or she shows in taking action. Thus, any actions should be mutually reviewed promptly, according to the outcome, client needs, and organizational values, to determine whether the employee went far enough or too far, or whether it was entirely appropriate to the situation, the customer, and the practice goals.

Cross-training and Sharing Responsibility

Employees should be cross-trained whenever possible. Granted, complete cross-training has practical limitations. Nevertheless, employees who perform the jobs of other staff members occasionally are more likely to cooperate with one another. If you can't truly rotate employees, try to free them to "shadow" another employee, or even you, for at least part of a day. Strong alliances may be forged by such an experience. Dr. Paul Glouton of Lilburn Animal Hospital in Lilburn, GA, explains:

> One of the major benefits is that each staff member begins to understand the others' difficulties. This is extremely helpful when we're very busy and someone forgets to follow protocol in minute detail. If, for instance, a receptionist doesn't get all the patient information in detail during a busy drop-off time, and the techs have worked the front desk during those times, they understand that the clients are frequently in a big hurry to get out the door and not always helpful in completing drop-off information.

In turn, after the receptionists have worked with the technicians, they understand how crucial this information can be.

> [An] incident that will be forever imprinted on one receptionist's brain was when a patient vomited its breakfast after surgery. The pet had supposedly not eaten breakfast, but… After the receptionist saw the staff in action to prevent aspiration of the vomitus, and the possible effects had the pet aspirated, she will never forget to double-check the status of an empty

*stomach. As a result of her experience, now all of
our receptionists double check as to the status of
surgery patients' previous meals.*

Dr. Glouton points out to staff members that they will
be considered more valuable if they have more than one
usable skill within the hospital. He further notes that,
for cross-training to work well and be accepted, the
hospital must plan for cross-training time. Areas should
not be short-staffed, nor should those being cross-
trained be expected to perform as though they were
regular staff members. "That's unfair to all and can
quickly sour the staff's commitment to cross-training. It
should be viewed as fun and mind-expanding, not
stressful and terrifying, to a committed staff member."

Business and clinical issues should be shared with the
entire staff. Too often, business issues stay in the front
office and clinical problems stay in the back. The whole
practice is affected by both issues, though, and
employees will work as a team more effectively if they
understand this. Some hospitals hold quarterly "state-of-
the-practice" meetings during which revenues, expenses,
and other financial issues are discussed with all staff
members.

Employees should also have a say in purchases they will
use. For instance, you might allow employees who will
work with your computer to participate in research and
decision making on the type of software you'll buy. After
all, your receptionist will probably use the software
much more often than you will. It's in your best interest
to ensure that the receptionist is comfortable with the
software you choose.

Standing Behind Your Employees

Empowerment tells your employees, "I trust you. I have
confidence in you." It gives them control, which can be
powerful. For empowerment to work effectively and to
provide the results you want (satisfied clients), several
factors should be present:

✦ Leaders and managers who believe in the ability of
   their staff to exercise judgment and self-control

✦ Employees who have strong needs to grow and test their personal competencies on the job

✦ A group of employees who function as a team, caring about each other as well as the customer

✦ Employees who understand the philosophy of the practice as well as their tasks

✦ Employee problem-solving and teamwork skills

✦ An atmosphere of confidence in individuals and teams

✦ A nonpunitive attitude toward mistakes

✦ Accepted practice service standards that guide behaviors and decisions (See Chapter 6.)

✦ Strong employee training and clear job descriptions

✦ Ongoing staff education for personal and professional development and more informed decision making

✦ Encouragement, implementation, and recognition of ideas and suggestions from employees at all levels

✦ Employees having a stake in the success and growth of the practice through profit-sharing, advancement opportunities, rewards, and recognition

Effective empowerment requires a leader who stands behind his or her employees. As a leader and team member, your employees rely on you to carry out what you say. A relief veterinarian describes a practice in which the receptionist was clearly confused about her boss' instructions:

> *I was told by the departing veterinarian that all clients were to pay at the time of their visit, and so I assumed that this was a standard policy. When I gave one client an estimate, though, she insisted that she always charged. The receptionist, looking confused, gave in to the client's request. Later she told me that she'd tried to enforce the policy, but the doctor would sometimes come to the front desk and tell certain clients that they could charge after all. Although she tried to enforce his policy, he under-mined her efforts and left her always wondering which clients would be the exception today. What's*

more, she ended up looking like the "bad guy" to the clients, who learned to pressure the doctor for special treatment.

The practice owner would have been better off to stay in the back room and let his receptionist do her job, which would include giving clients a tactful reminder about the payment policy at the time they made their appointments.

To avoid such pitfalls, the practice owner should provide a threat-free atmosphere in which the staff can work. "Threat-free" doesn't mean "without consequences," though. It means a positive atmosphere in which employees aren't punished for taking risks and doing their jobs right. A threat-free environment encourages disclosure and discussion of embarrassing or sensitive behaviors, even (or especially) on the part of the veterinarians. It also encourages innovation because mistakes, the natural consequence of creative thinking, are not punished. They're regarded as growth bumps!

Dr. Thomas Austin knows (and shows his staff) that a threat-free environment encourages input. He demonstrates that he's not just listening by following through with action.

> *One summer we were busier than all get-out and everyone wasn't real happy; there were a lot of undercurrents of problems. We got the whole staff together and went away from the hospital in the evening. We had asked for staff feedback going into the meeting, and we had one letter that was very negative, so we read the letter and everyone applauded the person who wrote it. Then we all sat down and re-formed our mission statement and started all over again. We're still going. There are always going to be problems, but we are doing our level best to get them addressed.*

Empowering Through Ownership

Employees will understand the limits and responsibilities of empowerment when they observe you consistently acting out a client-centered service philosophy. (Remember what we said about leadership?) Encourage and use employee input and ideas. This is a strong motivator. People own what they create.

At the Broadway Animal Hospital, veterinary technician Carol Gaffney takes responsibility for client satisfaction: "I see myself as the client advocate, making sure the client doesn't fall through the cracks and making sure the client stays informed and comfortable through the whole process."[6]

When you generate problems to be solved or when you ask for staff involvement, provide resources — time as well as materials. When an employee's action saves the practice money or brings in extra income, give the employee an "instant bonus" commensurate with the savings or action. Include a personal note of thanks. When reinforcement occurs simultaneously with the behavior, as psychologist B.F. Skinner discovered with his research many years ago, the behavior continues.

Encourage staff members to recognize each other's efforts. Lilburn Animal Hospital uses a monthly KUDOS award consisting of a $50 gift certificate to promote positive thoughts and actions. Any staff member, including the veterinarians, may be nominated at any time by another staff member for going above and beyond the expected to help a client, patient, the hospital, or another staff member. Dr. Glouton notes that recent awards were given for a receptionist who took a pet home to an elderly client who could not come to pick it up; to a technician who worked on her day off so a sick staff member could go home; and to a doctor for talking late into the night with a client who had recently euthanized a pet, helping that person seek professional counseling.

As the service quality of practices escalates, so do the demands on employees. To help the staff learn appropriate ways to deal with situations and problems, review situations as soon as possible after they occur, and discuss a variety of ways to handle them. This is typical in client-centered practices. In staff meetings and small group meetings, role playing and situation analysis give employees specific, hands-on understanding of acceptable responses.

Achieving Lasting Benefits

Does empowerment yield results? It depends on the kind of results you seek in your practice. If your goal is a client-centered practice, take a look at organizations with highly empowered employees: Nordstrom, the Ritz-Carlton Hotel Company, Marriott, and Federal Express. All are companies renowned for their quality of service. For example, at Ritz-Carlton, a National Baldridge Quality Award winner, employees are empowered to "move heaven and earth" to resolve the problems of a guest. Intensive and ongoing training provides the hotel's staff with the ability to make these heaven-and-earth decisions. In addition to a 3-day orientation for new staff members, Ritz-Carlton has daily "line-ups" in each department, during which time information is passed from one shift to another. Empowered staff members are rewarded with instant recognition, such as the Lightning Strikes Award, which can be given to any employee who goes above and beyond the call of duty in service to a guest or a coworker (Figure 8.2).[7]

Even though empowerment requires an investment of trust, its benefits are specific and lasting. An article in *Sloan Management Review* lists these outcomes[8]:

✦ Quicker responses to customer needs during service delivery

✦ Quicker responses to dissatisfied customers during service recovery

✦ Employees who feel better about their jobs and themselves

✦ Employees who interact with customers with more warmth and enthusiasm

✦ Employees who are a source of ideas about how to best serve the customer

✦ Employees who provide word-of-mouth advertising and customer retention

Empowerment improves productivity, veterinarian and staff efficiency and effectiveness, and client satisfaction. Learning to empower employees wisely is a delicate skill, requiring balance between too much and not enough. The overloaded, harried practitioner may be tempted to

Figure 8.2 The Ritz-Carlton® Credo

The Ritz-Carlton® Hotel is a place where the genuine care and comfort of our guests is our highest mission.
We pledge to provide the finest personal service and facilities for our guests, who will always enjoy a warm, relaxed, yet refined ambience.
The Ritz-Carlton® experience enlivens the senses, instills well-being, and fulfills even the unexpressed wishes and needs of our guests.

The Ritz-Carlton® Basics

1. The Credo will be known, owned, and energized by all employees.
2. Our motto is: "We are Ladies and Gentlemen serving Ladies and Gentlemen." Practice teamwork and "lateral service" to create a positive work environment.
3. The three steps of service shall be practiced by all employees.
4. All employees will successfully complete Training Certification to ensure they understand how to perform to The Ritz-Carlton® standard in their position.
5. Each employee will understand their work area and Hotel goals as established in each strategic plan.
6. All employees will know the needs of their internal and external customers (guests and employees) so that we may deliver the products and services they expect. Use guest preference pads to record specific needs.
7. Each employee will continuously identify defects (Mr. BIV) throughout the Hotel.
8. Any employee who receives a customer complaint "owns" the complaint.
9. Instant guest pacification will be ensured by all. React quickly to correct the problem immediately. Follow-up with a telephone call within twenty minutes to verify the problem has been resolved to the customer's satisfaction. Do everything you possibly can to never lose a guest.
10. Guest incident action forms are used to record and communicate every incident of guest dissatisfaction. Every employee is empowered to resolve the problem and to prevent a repeat occurrence.
11. Uncompromising levels of cleanliness are the responsibility of every employee.
12. "Smile—We are on stage" Always maintain positive eye contact. Use the proper vocabulary with our guests. (Use worlds like—"Good Morning, " "Certainly," "I'll be happy to," and "My pleasure").
13. Be an ambassador of your Hotel in and outside of the work place. Always talk positively. No negative comments.

14. Escort guests rather than pointing out directions to another area of the Hotel.
15. Be knowledgeable of Hotel information (hours of operation, etc.) to answer guest inquiries. Always recommend the Hotel's retail and food and beverage outlets prior to outside facilities.
16. Use proper telephone etiquette. Answer within three rings and with a "smile." When necessary, ask the caller, "May I place you on hold?" Do not screen calls. Eliminate call transfers when possible.
17. Uniforms are to be immaculate: Wear proper and safe footwear (clean and polished), and your correct name tag. Take pride and care in your personal appearance (adhering to all grooming standards).
18. Ensure all employees know their role during emergency situations and are aware of fire and life safety response processes.
19. Notify your supervisor immediately of hazards, injuries, equipment, or assistance that you need. Practice energy conservation and proper maintenance and repair of Hotel property and equipment.
20. Protecting the assets of a Ritz-Carlton® hotel is the responsibility of every employee.

The Three Steps of Service

1. A warm and sincere greeting: Use the guest's name, if and when possible.
2. Anticipation and compliance with guest needs.
3. Fond farewell: Give them a warm goodbye, and use their names if and when possible.

Source: © The Ritz-Carlton Hotel Company, 1983. Ritz-Carlton® materials were provided by The Ritz-Carlton Hotel Company. The Ritz-Carlton® is a federally registered trademark of The Ritz-Carlton Hotel Company.

delegate tasks wholesale without training or follow-up. The result can vary from excellent to something as drastic as embezzlement and fraud. Anyone who has had a taste of the latter is more than a little hesitant to turn loose the keys to the coffee maker, much less the keys to the front door!

At the other end of the spectrum, employees have extremely limited capabilities. Think of the client's reaction to, "Sure, I can fix that billing error" compared to, "I'm sorry, I'll have to check with my supervisor, and he's out for a week. Check back with us later."

Investing in The Team

Companies that retain employees also retain customers–Ross Clark, DVM[9]

You must select, hire, and train employees carefully to give them responsibility and authority. This initial investment in the selection saves in the long run, though. You'll have less turnover when staffers truly fit their assignments and feel comfortable carrying out the philosophy of the practice. Granted, labor costs may be higher: Rather than paying minimum wage (and getting a minimum wage mentality and attitude), you must pay more for intelligent, personable people. Over time, though, these higher-salaried employees pay their way in productivity.

Changing the "not my job" attitude to "I'll take care of it" isn't without a few potholes into which you and your employees may occasionally stumble. If you've hired the right people, given them the best foundation, and kept up the coaching, though, you may frequently hear clients say: "Doctor, you've got such a great bunch of people. I feel like I can ask them anything!" And you and your clients will hear this sweet-sounding phrase a lot more often: "Sure, I can take care of it!"

Notes

1. M. Landsberg. *The Tao of Coaching: Boost your effectiveness by inspiring those around you.* Santa Monica, CA: Knowledge Exchange, 1997: 30–31
2. A. Ashby. Communication Is Key to This Practice's Success. *AAHA Trends*, May 1993:15–16.
3. Landsberg.
4. R. Zemke and D. Schaaf. *The Service Edge: 101 Companies That Profit from Customer Care.* New York: New American Library, 1989: 66–67.
5. C. Handy. Balancing Corporate Power: A New Federalist Paper. *Harvard Business Review*, Nov/Dec 1992: 59–72.
6. S. Brown et al. *Patient Satisfaction Pays: Quality Service for Practice Success.* Gaithersburg, MD: Aspen Publications, 1993: 116–117
7. Brown et al.
8. D. E. Bowen and E. E. Lawler, III. The Empowerment of Service Workers: What, Why, How, and When. *Sloan Management Review*, 33(3) (Spring 1992): 31–39.
9. R. Clark. *Mastering the Marketplace: Taking Your Practice to the Top.* Lenexa, KS: Veterinary Medicine Publishing Group, 1996.

Action Steps for Empowering Your Staff

1. Build employee confidence with information, educational opportunities, and organizational values and standards.

2. Set forth clear expectations.

3. Provide comprehensive training, including manuals covering practice rules, policies, instructions, and protocols, plus a new-employee mentor. Cross-train employees.

4. Hold people accountable for areas of responsibility and actions.

5. Set limits and decision-making parameters.

6. Praise in public and criticize in private.

7. Believe and trust in your employees' abilities.

8. Review "empowered" employee actions according to outcome, client needs, and organizational values.

9. Chart and act on ideas that employees suggest for improving service.

Chapter 9

Continuing Education— for Veterinarians and Staff

If a practice spends 2% to 5% of its annual payroll on employee training, it should realize about a 10% increase in net profit.[1]

Today, a well-trained staff isn't a luxury; it's a requirement. New clients see and assess your staff long before they rate your expertise.[2]

How do you go about educating yourself and your staff? Do you think continuing education is just for veterinarians? As we've said, an investment in staff training is an essential component of empowerment. We talked about basic training for your staff in the last chapter. Once you've educated employees about their fundamental job duties, though, there's still room for improvement.

When we speak of continuing education, we mean education of the entire veterinary team. We also mean education in all areas—technical, medical, and surgical expertise, and also practice management and quality service. Client satisfaction depends on it. In this chapter we present some ideas for delivering quality service *and* quality medicine in your practice.

Committing to Education

Many practices hold regular educational sessions for staff on clinical, personal, and team-building topics. Emphasizing a variety of educational topics acknowledges to your staff that you regard them as complete and complex individuals, not just "workers." ServiceMaster, the "housekeeping" company for business, allows employees to attend classes on company time in personal finance, stress management, and other subjects.

According to a ServiceMaster vice president, "Our root motivator for committing so much time, money and effort to training is the company's second corporate objective: to use our business as a tool to help people grow and develop."[3] The company has found that education motivates low-level employees to move up to high-level, even managerial, openings.[3] Education enhances participation and self-esteem for everyone, not to mention increasing your staff's knowledge and ability to make decisions!

The Safari Animal Care Center of League City, TX, sends its staff to continuing education meetings, then has them develop lesson plans and make presentations during subsequent staff meetings. Michelin Mauldin, head of client relations, says, "When given the opportunity to grow, people get excited about their jobs. Clients recognize that excitement and feel they're part of something special. And that keeps them coming back."[4]

By showing your commitment to your staff, you are showing your commitment to client satisfaction and quality service. You might host seminars at the clinic and send employees to outside conferences when these would be beneficial. Many conferences offer more than clinical seminars. Their programs focus on the entire hospital team, including receptionists, technicians, and practice managers.

We were impressed with the number of staff development opportunities offered by the practices we visited. Many devote at least one afternoon a month to formal educational programs in addition to short breakfast and lunchtime sessions and other "feed the brain" get-togethers. If you do the same, your investment will be returned in improved productivity and a renewed sense of teamwork. You can encourage ongoing learning by circulating books, articles, audiotapes, and videotapes to staff members and by including discussions of hot topics and interesting articles in meetings.

Who's the Technician Around Here?

Dr. Peggy Rucker, hospital director at Southwest Virginia Veterinary Services in Lebanon, VA, is committed to staff education. She sends her technicians, receptionist, and practice manager to gatherings such as the AAHA national meeting.

"I felt it was important to go to a large national meeting where there was so much education available," Dr. Rucker said. She knows that educated technicians are better informed, which promotes client interaction. "My clients are educated before I go in the exam room, and that's because my technicians spend a lot of time explaining procedures and answering questions."[5]

Are you spending half your time performing tasks that could be done by a certified veterinary technician? Do you really think you got your point across about flea control the tenth time you said the same thing in one day? Veterinarians who insist on being involved in taking radiographs, drawing blood, running laboratory tests, or doing all the nutrition and flea control counseling are headed toward burnout and aren't doing their clients a favor.

Successful veterinarians know their technicians are talented, knowledgeable professionals. When they free up their own time by delegating technical tasks, these veterinarians can focus on expanding their knowledge of preventive medicine, diagnosis, and treatment to benefit each animal that comes to their practices.

Investing in Staff Education

Writes Mark Opperman, CVPM:

Sending a technician to a conference conveys the message that you regard that person as a professional in whom you're willing to invest. If you're not willing to spend time and money training your team, you're not investing in your practice's future.

*Continuing education enhances your employees'
self-image and fosters a team approach that
improves the quality of service you provide to clients
and patients.*[6]

Staff education not only enhances job performance but
also saves you money, improves client satisfaction, and
eases your workload. Educated staff members can answer
many of your clients' routine health care questions. Use
AAHA's *Commonly Asked Questions Reference Guide* to
discuss client questions with staff members and to
develop your recommended answers. Or have your
receptionist and technician come up with their own lists
of common client questions, then discuss the appropriate answers during a staff meeting.

Your team might attend city, state, or regional continuing education and practice management meetings. If
you, one of your technicians, and the practice manager
all attend the same large meeting, imagine how much
more information you'll bring back to the practice! And
imagine how much more easily you can implement
changes when you involve staff members in what you
learn. Many practices hold staff meetings following
continuing education seminars, where staff members
present what they learned to fellow staff members.

When you return from a national conference or continuing education program or when you start performing
a new test or procedure, review with your staff what
you've learned and its significance to clients. When you
purchase new equipment, educate those who will be
using it, and also make certain that everyone in the
hospital understands how the equipment benefits the
practice and clients.

Keeping Up

And what about you, the veterinarian? Like others you
know, you attend continuing education meetings
regularly—but is that enough? Do you spend as much
time learning as you do visiting? Do you keep up with
new technology and equipment, and use the Internet to
acquire information on medicine and surgery?

Let's hope your clients aren't like a pet owner from
Ramona, California, who says that if her pet were in a

life-threatening situation, she'd bypass her regular doctor: "I'd go to the vet in town who charges more; she's better."[7]

You may know of a veterinarian who is personable, affable, and brilliant when it comes to the business side of veterinary practice. He or she may have a busy practice, yet his or her surgical skills leave much to be desired. Educated clients learn to look beyond the friendly face and ask questions about medical and surgical procedures. What's more, friendly but incompetent veterinarians can't fool their own staff for long, so they end up with higher turnover and lower service quality as a result.

To avoid that scenario, improve your skills through continuing education, veterinary and professional journals, and collegial consultation and discussion. Formal continuing education meetings aren't the only way to brush up on your medical skills and knowledge. Veterinarians in many cities form "journal clubs," which meet once or twice a month to discuss current journal articles. Others attend breakfast meetings where they hash over the details of tough cases, or they participate in "grand rounds," where they share new knowledge from continuing education courses with other veterinarians in the community.

Thousands of veterinarians are realizing the benefit of using electronic mail and the Internet to get quick responses from specialists when they need help with difficult cases. These kinds of frequent interactions are especially crucial for solo practitioners.

Knowing Your Limitations

[At veterinary continuing education meetings] most practitioners gravitate toward subjects that interest them, but we miss the point of true continuing education by not attending lectures on unfamiliar topics.—Dr. Susan Coe[8]

Be aware of your limitations as well as your capabilities. Devote as much time to studying your weak areas as you do to your special interests. Veterinarians like Dr. Paul Glouton regularly utilize the services of specialists.

*We're able to contact a board-certified internal
medicine specialist for consultation by pager at any
time. He also comes to our office for a day every
other week to review selected cases, and to have a 1-
hour discussion on an article in a refereed journal or
topic of our choice. We find this money well spent in
providing leading-edge medicine to our clients. The
clients win with better medical care, and we win by
furthering our own education. It's a positive boost to
staff morale to know we are providing the best and
latest care available.*

Improving computer technology and a gradual reduction
in its cost will allow increasing use of "telemedicine," or
the digitizing of medical information for transmittal to a
specialist in another location. Veterinarians who are
able to offer this kind of service will further enhance
client satisfaction and their own medical expertise. As
Dr. Robert Cartin of Mission Animal & Bird Hospital in
Oceanside, CA, says:

*People feel good when we say we're going to send
films off to surgeons or radiologists for other opinions. Sometimes specialists come back with a
recommendation and they or we will talk to the
client about that. There are times when we just
bring in another one of our own doctors to see what
he or she thinks about a case, taking advantage of
the fact that we are a multiple-doctor practice.*

Knowing your capabilities and limitations includes
knowing when to refer. Know when you're not ready for
a new procedure, when you don't know enough about a
new drug, or when you've reached the limits of your
knowledge about a certain condition. When necessary,
refer your clients to the experts. Know who they are and
what their skills are, as well as their limitations. Be
honest with yourself as well as with your clients.

Wise veterinarians are comfortable admitting when
they're beyond their capabilities. They realize it's just as
important to admit what they don't know as it is to act
proficiently when they do know how to proceed. They
enjoy directing clients to specialists, and their clients
respect them for doing so. Difficult cases have better

outcomes and the veterinarian benefits from learning new information with each incident. Ultimately, this is the best way to satisfy clients and to provide quality service.

Benchmarking: What You Can Learn from Others

You get your medical and surgical education by learning from specialists in those areas. But how do you get continuing education credits in *service*? Chances are that you attend veterinary practice management seminars and you've sent your staff members to their share of educational meetings (or you will, now that you've gotten this far!). But do you limit your education to what's offered in the veterinary field? Educating yourself and your staff needn't be limited to your own profession. Many veterinarians have borrowed customer-service ideas from other businesses and are using them in meeting, greeting, and treating their clients.

Providing service that is outstanding, memorable, and customer-focused has long been a competitive business strategy for nonveterinary organizations. Among the companies that have built success on service, one that stands out is Nordstrom, the Seattle-based department store, which will go to any length to accommodate a customer's needs. Nordstrom knows that customer loyalty stems from its service orientation. Noting this and other examples of extraordinary service, you might want to discuss with your staff how you can apply some of their ideas to your practice.

We know this is a paradigm shift for many in veterinary practice, and it requires stepping out of your traditional veterinary box to make the shift. It's not easy. You may believe that consumerism has jaded many people's view of veterinarians. Consumerism, however, is not to be blamed for the tenuous nature of some veterinarian-client relationships. Rather, the failure comes from not acknowledging the critical role of this relationship in the veterinary encounter.

Benchmarking once was a technical term that denoted a surveyor's reference point. In the quality-focused corporate world, it refers to adopting or adapting the best practices and strategies for a specific activity from other businesses and industries. Or, as quality guru Juran defines it, "setting goals based on knowing what has been achieved by others." [9] He points out that benchmarking implies that the goal is attainable because others already have achieved it. Benchmarking is an effective tool for improvement in service quality because the "reference points" are everywhere.

Perhaps you've begun to realize that your clients are comparing your practice, sometimes unfavorably, with doctors, dentists, and even the restaurants and retail stores they patronize. Customers like the personal attention they get from the salesclerk at Nordstrom, from the service advisor at the Saturn dealership, and from the friendly waitress at the coffee shop around the corner who knew long before the advent of total quality management that paying attention to her customers pays off in bigger tips as well as a more enjoyable work day.

Customers—your clients—have learned that they don't have to accept poor service. Their expectations have escalated as service standards have risen (unfortunately not uniformly; there's still plenty of poor service around), and they bring these rising expectations into your practice.

Continuing Education for Service

You can familiarize yourself with what other industries are doing to improve customer service and to increase satisfaction by reading about them. Publications such as *Fortune, Forbes, Business Week, USA Today,* and *Inc.,* as well as bestselling books on this topic, explore the latest service trends as well as time-tested techniques for satisfying customers and improving business productivity and efficiency. Read, share, and use information in books and articles that may be applicable to your practice.

Also, pay attention to service experiences when you travel, dine, or shop. Read magazines you ordinarily don't read. Encourage staff members to bring up ideas and encounters from outside of veterinary medicine. When you experience "service fanaticism" in your daily life, whether it is at the dry cleaners, the supermarket, or your bank, pay attention to what happens, how, why, and who provides it. Tell the story of your experience to your staff, and ask employees to share their stories about similar encounters. That will emphasize to them that you take service seriously and show what a strong impact service extras can have. Your client loyalty will flourish if clients sense a strong, sincere, and personalized service attitude on the part of everyone in the practice.

Walk into any Gap store, and you'll be assaulted with ideas any practice could adapt. The first thing that happens is a friendly greeting from a good-natured salesperson, who may ask, "What do you think of our new colors?" instead of the more typical and impersonal "May I help you?" This prompts a response from the customer that is quite different from the usual, "No thanks; I'm just looking."

At the Gap, Nordstrom, and other service-focused businesses, employees know their product and show it with service. Ask a question, and the service personnel at these stores have the answer. On the rare occasions when they don't, they'll find an answer for you— quickly.

Are your staff members familiar with all the services you provide and your client-care philosophy? Can they answer clients' questions about whether you do blood glucose tests in-house, how often you recommend blood chemistry screens for dogs over age 12, your policy on returning phone calls, or your stance on the new leuke- mia vaccine?

We don't intend to trivialize veterinary medicine by comparing it to retail sales. Instead, we urge you to focus on the *way* these companies deliver services, borrowing the aspects you can apply to your own practice to better satisfy your clients.

When you borrow ideas, though, restrain yourself. Some veterinarians have gotten carried away by the marble and expensive furnishings they encounter in exclusive resort lobbies. The result is benchmarking excess. As one client commented when he walked into a plush waiting room: "Do I have to pay for this?"

Borrowing ideas successfully requires common sense and knowledge of your clients. As with any other educational process, you can use the information most useful to you and put aside the rest until you need it. When you incorporate benchmarking into your continuing education plan, you improve service and client satisfaction while widening the horizons of everyone in the practice.

Notes

1. R. Gerson. *Beyond Customer Service: Keeping Clients for Life*. Menlo Park, CA: Crisp Publications/AVMA, 1994: 49–50.
2. R. Clark. *Mastering the Marketplace: Taking Your Practice to the Top*. Lenexa, KS: Veterinary Medicine Publishing Group, 1996:16.
3. Focus on...ServiceMaster. *Service Edge*, Feb 1992: 3.
4. C. Cook. An Investment That Pays. *Veterinary Economics*, Apr 1997: 64–70.
5. M. Knudsen. Commit to Your Technician's Education. *AAHA Trends*, Sep 1994:19-20.
6. M. Opperman. Continuing Education: It's Not Just for Doctors Anymore. *Veterinary Economics*, Oct 1996: 76–79.
7. American Animal Hospital Association. *1995 AAHA Report: A Study of the Companion Animal Veterinary Services Market*: 111.
8. C. Chapman. Your Ticket to Learning. *Veterinary Economics*, May 1997: 72–74.
9. J. M. Juran. *Juran on Quality by Design: The New Steps for Planning Quality into Goods and Services*, New York: Free Press, 1992: 35.

Action Steps for Educating Yourself and Your Staff

1. Invest in educating your staff and use staff members to their full potential.

2. Get the most out of continuing education meetings by having several staff members and doctors attend, then having them present what they learned to the entire team.

3. Be prepared to provide clients with information to help them evaluate the expertise of doctors and staff members.

4. Evaluate your technical skills against available standards and know your capabilities and limitations.

5. Consult with specialists on difficult cases; refer your clients to experts with appropriate skills when necessary.

6. Pay attention to other industries, and learn from the customer-sensitive and service-oriented things they do.

7. Develop a network of experts in other industries with whom you can trade information and ideas.

8. Read the *Wall Street Journal, Fortune, Business Week,* and other business publications and bestselling books, as well as more specialized publications such as *Veterinary Economics, Trends,* and the *Journal of the American Veterinary Medical Association.*

9. Remember that your clients compare the service experiences they have with other businesses. Don't permit your own service to clients fall short of their experiences with other successful businesses.

Chapter 10

Suggestions for Practice Managers Only

I finally promoted my main receptionist to a practice manager/receptionist. Since I don't have a lot of time, she has come up with several ideas to improve client satisfaction. We have a client satisfaction survey we send out when someone wants records transferred. She has worked on a Christmas mailing list and clinic newsletter. She is always bringing client gripes and praise to my attention.—Dr. Mike Bellinghausen, Kenmore, WA

Throughout this book we talk about leadership, commitment, vision, goals, and objectives for achieving "super service" and client satisfaction. We've offered concepts and suggestions with the understanding that the veterinarian is our primary audience, for he or she is the person with the greatest potential influence in the practice.

We are pragmatists, though. We deal in reality, and so do you. We know that in some practices the practice manager or staff members are the driving force behind quality service and client satisfaction. Most of the innovative ideas are developed and put in place by the receptionist, bookkeeper, veterinary technician, or practice manager. The practice manager or staff must encourage the veterinarian(s) to communicate with clients, to educate them about their conditions, to spend an appropriate amount of time with them, and to meet their needs. So we wrote this chapter to help you.

Providing More Than Quality Medicine

The veterinarian in some practices is dedicated to quality veterinary care but not necessarily to the customer. As a result, the practice may be drifting. Clients come for their appointments not because they are committed to the practice and impressed with the level of caring attention they get but, rather, because it's too much trouble to change, or they like the staff, or because it's convenient. Amazingly enough, people will choose a veterinarian based solely on the fact that "the clinic was nearby and I saw the sign."

Some clients continue to come to practices in which service is secondary because their pets are healthy and the interaction with the practice or veterinarian is infrequent. Given a medical emergency, however, their views of the practice and the veterinarian might change significantly. Meanwhile, you know they're not giving favorable recommendations to their friends, coworkers, or anyone else they encounter. The result is that the practice isn't growing. You're frustrated because you know Dr. Michaels is a good veterinarian. You know he cares. You know that if you could just get him motivated, get him to understand the importance to clients and to the practice of providing excellent service, his attitude would change. The practice would be a better place for everyone: the veterinarian, the staff, and especially the clients.

How do you motivate the veterinarian, or several of them, to emphasize client satisfaction? How do you get veterinarians to become committed to providing excellent service along with excellent medical care?

Planning Your Strategy

Here's what you need to do. Read (or reread) Chapter 7, on motivating staff. The guidelines for getting the staff motivated and enthusiastic apply to anyone, including veterinarians. As you plan your strategy for motivating the veterinarians in your practice, keep the following principles in mind:

✦ Provide reasons for the veterinarians to want to improve client satisfaction. People do what they want to. You can't make them want something. What they want (what they respond to and are motivated by) must be consistent with their internal values and goals.

✦ Find a time to engage each of the veterinarians individually in conversation. Ask why they went into veterinary medicine. Their responses are quite likely to be similar to this: "I wanted to help people. I admired the dedication of doctors I encountered when I was young. I wanted to be able to do something for animals and people and feel good about it." If the veterinarians say that their reason for entering veterinary medicine was to give to others and to help animals, you've found a motivator. The desire to satisfy clients relates strongly to the "giving" value.

✦ Demonstrate actively your strong belief in quality service. Be enthusiastic no matter what the attitude or reaction of others. People are inspired and motivated by those who are passionate and show conviction.

✦ When you observe a veterinarian meeting or exceeding a client's expectations and you hear or observe the client's favorable reaction, mention casually to the veterinarian how pleased the client was. Put it in writing if appropriate. People respond to positive feedback no matter who they are or what their position or status.

✦ Demonstrate leadership through subtle (not subversive or deceitful) action. People follow leaders. In Chapter 5 we said that the veterinarian is the natural leader of the practice. Managers, administrators, and support staff, too, can provide quality leadership by example if the veterinarian is uninterested or reluctant.

You may need a variety of approaches. Most veterinarians respond to facts and data. They're oriented to research because of their background in medical education and clinical training. Seldom do they prescribe a drug or hospitalize a patient on the basis of a hunch. They run tests, take radiographs, perform biopsies, and review the medical history before they make a decision. They gather and rely on facts and data, then interpret them. You need to do the same.

Supporting Your Position

Armed with facts and data, you can prove with detailed information why a practice focus on client satisfaction through superior service will yield tangible benefits. The practice already may have evidence in client survey results, patient record transfer requests, percentage of client referrals, and the like. The references and citations throughout this book attest to the advantages of striving to achieve satisfaction from the client's perspective with every encounter and interaction.

One office manager in a practice of 20 physicians, most of whom are quality oriented, said she presents recalcitrant physicians with the need to improve client satisfaction by positioning it as a risk-management issue. She cites research studies that show reduced malpractice liability in practices with good communication and a high level of client satisfaction. "They need to hear it," she said.

Use the kind of data to which the veterinarians in your practice will respond. If you need dollars for the bottom-line doctor, use dollars. Use improvement in productivity for the veterinarian who is oriented toward productivity. Use professional pride and satisfaction for the veterinarian seeking that ethic. Use whatever is appropriate, or a combination. Support your argument with the kind of results that will get your audience's attention.

Put persuasive information (your facts and data) in a format to which the veterinarian will respond best. Some people respond to visual stimuli. If so, use plenty of diagrams, charts, and graphs, or perhaps a more formal presentation using slides or overhead transparencies. Some people are print-oriented and prefer a report (but make sure you go over it personally). More auditory veterinarians will appreciate a verbal rundown.

Provide ongoing support and backing for your argument. Clip or mark articles pertaining to the benefits of client satisfaction and service quality, and circulate them to those you are trying to persuade. Make sure that favorable notes and comments from clients about a positive interaction or experience in the practice go to the veterinarian as well as the staff. Call attention to these items during your regular meeting with the veterinarian if you suspect they may end up buried unnoticed under a pile of reading material. Discuss examples of extraordinary service you've encountered in other businesses, and how that influences you to remain a loyal customer.

Knowing How to Use Influence

Use the power of influence. The book *Influence: The New Psychology of Modern Persuasion* cites the following "weapons of influence" that can be used ethically to win someone over to your point of view:[1]

✦ *Reciprocation.* Make a deal with the veterinarian: "I'll try this change in the schedule you've been asking for if you'll try these two communication techniques with your clients." When you give someone something, the recipient feels an obligation to reciprocate. Start with a bigger request, and if you get a "no," scale it down to something smaller. You may just get a "yes."

✦ *Commitment and consistency:* People tend to act consistently with previous behavior. If you can get Dr. Michaels to agree to try some small change in his service quality behavior (and you then document favorable or positive results), you have a better chance of "upping the ante" when you suggest a related activity.

✦ *Social proof.* People want to do as their peer group does. Talk about and cite evidence of client satisfaction efforts in other practices in your community and elsewhere. Check with the AVMA, the AAHA, and *Trends* and *Veterinary Economics* magazines for documentation, examples, and specifics.

✦ *Authority.* Because people tend to respond to authority figures, cite evidence from veterinary leadership: the AVMA, city or state veterinary association officers, or any other individual or group our veterinarian respects.

✦ *Scarcity*: Use the scarcity principle to influence veterinarians to learn more about client satisfaction. For example, a seminar or meeting that features client satisfaction as a discussion topic might be of greater interest if Dr. Michaels were to learn that space allows only a few additional registrants ("This is a hot topic, and if you don't participate, Doctor, you're going to miss out on knowing what all your friends know").

Creating a Symphony with Veterinarians and Staff

The commitment and participation of the veterinarians is a vital component of a successful, lasting, quality service that results in satisfied clients as well as economic and professional fulfillment. When veterinarians and staff members work together in concert to make every client's experience as positive as possible, the effect is harmonious and lasting. Compare this concordant, cooperative approach to that of one person playing Beethoven's Fifth Symphony on the piano. The pianist can make beautiful, uplifting music, but when the whole orchestra—strings, woodwinds, and percussion instruments—joins in, following the lead of the conductor, the effect is stirring, satisfying, and memorable for performers and audience alike.

Notes

1. R. B. Cialdini. *Influence: The New Psychology of Modern Persuasion.* New York: Quill Publishing, 1984.

Action Steps for Practice Managers and Staff

1. Talk with the veterinarian to discover his or her personal motivators.

2. Actively demonstrate your enthusiastic belief in quality service.

3. Share comments from satisfied clients with the veterinarian.

4. Assemble facts and data about the tangible benefits of a practice focus on client satisfaction, and share the information in a format suited to the veterinarian's style.

5. Provide ongoing evidence of the benefits of client satisfaction.

6. Use the "weapons of influence" to convince the veterinarian of the advantages of a client-centered practice.

Part Three

Let's Get Specific: Service Improvement for Client Retention

You've developed a vision for your practice and surveyed your clients to find out what they expect. You've hired and trained employees you trust and empowered them with knowledge and responsibility. Now it's time to get down to the specifics of service improvement. How can you get new clients in the door and keep them coming back?

Your first contact with clients is via the telephone. Is yours answered promptly and courteously by knowledgeable employees? The client's next hurdle is your scheduling system. Are clients able to make appointments at convenient times? Once they arrive, are they seen on time?

After clients are seated in the exam room, how does your communication style affect their final appraisal of your practice? How can you create partnerships with your clients (give-and-take relationships that acknowledge the responsibility of both parties in the outcome of the pet's health care)?

We'll suggest some answers to these questions. And, finally, we'll address a myriad of other service improvement tips and client retention strategies. Keeping in touch with your clients between visits, creating wellness programs, handling difficult situations empathetically, and addressing client complaints promptly and effectively add up to a picture of extraordinary client service.

Chapter 11

"Veterinary Clinic, Please Hold . . ."

Ring-ring-ring.

Ring-ring-ring.

Ring-ring-ring.

"Veterinary clinic. Please hold."

You can spend many hours communicating to the staff your philosophy of personalized care and your belief in quality service. You can recognize considerate acts, reward extraordinary actions, and feel justifiable pride in sensitivity to clients.

All of this significant progress toward putting the customer first, however, can be chipped away by that all-too-common scenario: "Hold, please."

The telephone is a vital connection between your practice and a potential or actual client. Faceless, untouchable, and remote, the voice that comes through to the caller carries emotion and attitude. The voice says clearly what the practice is like, what you and your veterinarian colleagues are like. The way your telephone is answered helps set up client expectations.

What does it say when the caller hears the telephone ring…and ring …and ring again and again before a voice responds? What is transmitted to a client when the person on the other end sounds bored, uncaring, or rushed? What is suggested when the voice on the other end of the line is an answering-service employee who mispronounces the veterinarian's name and knows nothing about the practice? What is the message when the voice is not a person at all but, instead, an automated electronic maze requiring endless, confusing button pushing before the caller finally reaches a person? And what kind of service and veterinary care expectations might someone have after getting connected to your practice in any of these ways?

Telephone Courtesy

Pet owners often report that veterinarians' phone service needs improvement. What are these people unhappy about? Being put on hold too long, lack of courtesy by staff members or the answering service, and veterinarians' delays in returning calls are a few reasons. Some of those unhappy customers may become irritated or frustrated enough to quit calling. They'll look for a practice in which telephone communication is a priority. If they were shopping for a veterinarian, you'll never get a chance to impress them with your skills because they won't be coming in.

We empathize with the people who answer the telephone in a veterinary practice. It's a tough job. The lines ring continually. Each caller expects personal, immediate attention. Some want to describe their pet's problem, from diarrhea to itching, in infinite, intimate detail. Meanwhile, a client is standing at the front desk trying to get the receptionist's attention, the technician is standing at her shoulder with a question about the caller on line 3, and Dr. Burston is on line 5 waiting to speak to Dr. King. And we're saying the person answering the telephone should smile and be friendly?

We are. Especially because the telephone connection is faceless and impersonal, the voice at the other end—the voice of the practice—has to respond with a name and a helpful tone. To ensure that this is the case, the practice leadership and management must understand and respect the significant role and responsibility of the person who answers the phone. This means hiring enough people so someone always has the time and energy to give the telephone the attention it deserves without taking away attention from clients already in the clinic. It means hiring sharp, compassionate individuals who understand the impact they have and training those who answer the phone not only to handle calls appropriately but also to convey the values of the practice as well as the services available.

Clients of Front Range Veterinary Clinic in Lakewood, CO, notice the clinic's outstanding phone service. Owner Dr. Brett Sargent understands the importance of training staff members in phone skills. "We use a combination of AAHA videotapes and hands-on training, with examples set by experienced team members," he says.

Evaluation of Your Phone Service

How does your staff respond to calls for veterinary advice? Does your technician or someone truly qualified screen your calls? If a client has an after-hours emergency, what happens when he or she calls your office? Do you use a good answering service or forward calls to an emergency service?

To evaluate your practice, take the telephone test in Figure 11.1. Then find out what clients actually experience when they call your practice with a mystery shopper survey (see Figure 11.2). Have your spouse or a close friend place a call during business hours—posing as a client with questions about the practice, or to schedule an appointment, or asking for veterinary advice. Then have him or her call after hours to evaluate what transpires. The form in Figure 11.2 is provided for this person to document his or her responses and attitude. Explain the mystery shopper survey to your staff in a positive manner. Its use can stimulate a discussion about client expectations, first impressions, and techniques for managing multiple calls.

Is your telephone answered by staff members during the hours clients are most likely to call? Many people need to make telephone calls before they start work themselves, or on their lunch breaks. If your telephones are answered by a service during these times, you're making

> **Figure 11.1 A Telephone Test**
>
> *Is the telephone voice in your practice a friendly one? Use the following list of questions to evaluate telephone responsiveness in your practice and to identify potential problem areas.*
>
> 1. How much specific training in telephone etiquette is given to the person who answers the phones?
>
> 2. How much and what kind of information is given to the receptionist about the practice, the veterinarian(s), and the services provided?
>
> 3. How is the receptionist instructed to answer the phone?
>
> 4. What form of telephone triage instructions and training does your receptionist receive?
>
> 5. How many telephone calls does your clinic receive each day?
>
> 6. What are the reasons for these calls?
>
> 7. How are calls documented?
>
> 8. How often do clients complain about your telephone service, and what do they complain about?
>
> 9. Do you solicit client comments about your telephone service?

it difficult for clients to contact you. That's not the best way to start or continue a relationship. An added benefit of making your staff available for longer periods instead of relying on an answering service is that your incoming calls will be spaced more manageably.

Dr. Thomas Austin believes clients should be able to reach a staff member 24 hours a day.

> *Although we refer after-hours emergencies to an emergency clinic, we still have staff members here around the clock. We are a large hospital and couldn't leave the number of patients we have here unattended. Our answering machine refers people to the emergency clinic and also gives them a number to call to reach someone here.*

When you get a call at night or on weekends, how do you keep a record of it? You should keep a log of every call and have the information transcribed into the client's chart. To keep transcription time to a minimum,

Figure 11.2 Mystery Shopper Survey

Date _____ Time _____

Reason for call _____

Phone number called _____ Number of rings _____

How answered: _____

Put on hold? _____ If so, how long? _____

Transferred? _____ If so, to whom? _____

Rate the friendliness of the receptionist:

❑ excellent   ❑ good   ❑ fair   ❑ poor

Rate the helpfulness of the receptionist

❑ excellent   ❑ good   ❑ fair   ❑ poor

First available date of scheduled appointment _____

Were you asked about how you would pay, or given information about a

payment policy? _____

Did receptionist offer to send practice brochure or other information?

_____

Comments: _____

_____

use a separate sheet for each call, and have the sheet attached directly to the chart. This is critical for accurate, comprehensive documentation, and it also conveys to clients a continuity in their pets' care, no matter what time of day or night.

Who Answers Your Telephone?

Is your receptionist overloaded with dual tasks of answering the phone and greeting clients? A receptionist who is on the phone when a client approaches the reception desk should always acknowledge the client with a nod or wave and eye contact. If it is anticipated that the phone call will take more than a few minutes, the receptionist might ask if he or she could call the person back at a less busy time, or ask the caller to hold a *brief* moment so the receptionist can get the client started on paperwork. Frequent interruptions signal the need for additional staffing.

Dr. Sargent solves the problem this way:

> *We have two receptionists who work together answering the phone and dealing with the front-desk duties. If they are snowed under, they usually will ask for help with the phone. Our kennel people and technical staff are expected to help when needed. All of our staff has been cross-trained.*

Training and adequate numbers of people are not enough to get the job done, though. Dr. Sargent adds:

> *The most important thing is to hire and keep good staff people. Most of our staff has been with us a long time. When you keep staff a long time, they learn your business quite well and get to know your clients very well. They become quite an asset. Clients love to be recognized on the phone or in person, and only experienced staff can do a good job of this.*

Do you use an informational recording or provide music for people put on hold? Do this with caution. Clients become irritated if they think they're left on hold for the sole purpose of listening to an advertisement. Recordings may be perceived as impersonal in spite of your good intentions. If you're not sure, ask your clients what they prefer. The goal is still to have brief, if any, "on hold" time.

Special Techniques and Skills

It makes me sick to even call my vet (whom I like overall). If I call the office to make an appointment, they pull my file and then when I come in, they can't ever find the file. It's gone or missing. So I always say, "Hey, since I called to make an appointment and you pulled my file, maybe it is in that huge stack of files waiting to be filed" (and there is always a mountain of files on top of the filing cabinets that never get filed). So then they dig and dig through those unfiled files until they find my file. It's a real hassle and frustrating too!

If your phones ring constantly and callers are frequently put on hold, or if your receptionist has trouble keeping up with other basic duties, your practice may require additional phone lines, more personnel to answer them, or better staff training. Most phone companies offer a service to identify peak busy periods for incoming calls; they also can determine how often callers are turned away with a busy signal. Either problem can be adjusted with more staff handling calls during busy periods or by adding a phone line if necessary.

A mature, well-trained telephone receptionist also can handle calls efficiently, taking care of callers quickly while maintaining a congenial, helpful tone. In many practices, unfortunately, the person who answers the phone is a minimally educated, minimally trained, minimum-wage individual. The technical skills are there. The employee knows all about picking up the handpiece and pushing the right buttons, but the important concepts of service, responsiveness, and attitude are missing. It's not the employee's fault. If no one conveys that the receptionist is the focal point for connecting clients to the practice, this employee may short-circuit clients and the practice because of lack of training and awareness.

The Phone Voice

Telephone conversations are more difficult than face-to-face interactions because the telephone poses a barrier that can impede communication. You can standardize telephone interactions without depersonalizing them, though (see Table 11.1). These are the minimum customer service requirements:

✦ The telephone receptionist should be taught (and believe) that he or she is the voice of the practice.

✦ Phones should be answered within three rings.

✦ The name of the practice or the veterinarian(s) should be given.

✦ The person answering the phone should give his or her first name.

✦ No caller should be put on hold without first being asked for permission.

Here's an example of acceptable handling:

Receptionist: Seaside Veterinary Hospital. This is Anna. Can you hold for a moment, please?

Caller: Yes, I can.

Anna: Thank you.

Unacceptable: "Seaside Veterinary Hospital. Hold please."

Those Pesky Intercoms

Does your receptionist put callers on hold and then leave the desk to find a technician or doctor? Do your staff members know how to use the telephone's intercom system, or is it going to waste? Does anyone know where the instruction manual is located? How much time does your staff waste running around finding each other, or you, to ask a question or relay information?

The intercom system is underused in many practices because no one knows how to use it. Have your practice manager dig out the instruction manual and set aside a few minutes to brief everyone on intercom use. Post a small card near each telephone with intercom tips. (Clients may be able to overhear intercom communications, so what you say should be moderated accordingly.)

Telephone Triage Protocol

A triage policy for handling phone calls helps to avoid an ongoing communication problem—or, worse, a malpractice situation. Develop a written telephone triage protocol with your receptionist. When multiple telephone calls come in, or when the waiting room is full of clients wondering when their turn will come (or if

Table 11.1 Knocking Down Telephone Barriers

Barrier	Action
Facial expressions, attitudes, and enunciation aren't clear	Speak clearly and at a moderate rate. Provide written material to follow up complex discussions.
Distractions deter listening and understanding	Focus on the caller. The person answering the phone should not attempt (or be required) to attend to other matters at the same time. Co-workers should keep background noise to a minimum and not interrupt the person on the phone.
Rapport is lacking	Give your voice personality; identify yourself by name. Smile while talking. Use a friendly, conversational tone; be calm and helpful. Use the client's name in conversation. If a call must be put on hold, ask permission first. If you use call waiting, never make your first caller wait more than a few seconds to answer a second incoming call. Give the second caller a choice of being called back or being put on hold.

they need to go outside and phone you to get your attention), this triage will help you avoid chaos.

The protocol, posted by every telephone, lists symptoms or problems that constitute emergencies requiring immediate attention, questions that can be answered only by a veterinarian, and questions that can be answered by a technician, an assistant, or other staff member.

Telephone Triage Protocol

1. List signs or conditions commonly seen in practice that require an immediate appointment or response by the veterinarian or technician.

2. Develop a written protocol for prescription refills, covering:

   ✦ Who can approve refills

   ✦ List of medications okay to refill without appointment and number of refills allowed

   ✦ Conditions or circumstances that require an appointment or lab tests before a refill

   ✦ Who takes questions about medications and reactions to medication

3. Develop a list of commonly asked questions and appropriate responses. Emphasize that additional questions not on the protocol list should be referred to the appropriate staffer.

The triage protocol should also list policies for prescription refills and for documentation of telephone calls. To establish a protocol, gather staffers who handle client calls and have them name the questions that are most commonly or frequently asked. (You may wish to have those who take client calls regularly keep a log of the questions for a week or two.) Make a list of the 10 or 20 most common questions, and specify appropriate answers or to whom the call should be referred. This saves time and pleases clients because answers often can be given immediately.

Callers who wish to speak to a veterinarian always should receive a "yes" reply to their request, even if the doctor is not immediately available. Although *you* may know that a staffer is capable of answering a client's question, clients don't like to feel that they're being passed off to someone else. Give them several choices, including the option to speak to a technician, to have a question relayed by the receptionist to the doctor, or to wait for a return call from the doctor (with an honest assessment of when that's likely to happen). By telling them "yes," followed by several options, you'll find that they often agree to talk with a staffer for the time being. Try this:

Yes, you may speak to Dr. Goldstein. However, she's treating a dog right now. Would you like to relay your question through Sally, our technician? She may be able to answer your question, and if not, she'll be sure to have the doctor call you back this afternoon.

Callbacks

Clients who are displeased with telephone courtesy in their veterinarians' offices are often unhappy with the amount of time the veterinarian or technician takes to return their phone calls. Some veterinarians take client calls throughout the day, but this approach may not work for you. A practice telephone policy can solve the problem.

The staff should know each veterinarian's schedule or time for returning phone calls to clients. Many veterinarians return calls at midday and at the end of the day. If a client calls at 8:30 a.m. with a nonemergency question and is informed politely that the doctor will return the call between noon and 2 p.m., the client knows that he or she doesn't have to sit by the phone waiting for the call. If the veterinarian prefers to return calls throughout the day between client appointments, the staff should be instructed to tell clients, "Dr. Avery makes client calls in between appointments. He can call you back sometime between now and noon. Is that convenient?" Managing return phone calls is similar to managing waiting time: Clients simply want to be informed and know what to expect.

Phone Shoppers

What's your success rate for bringing phone shoppers in to your clinic? Veterinarians who train their receptionists to focus on these calls find that their appointment rates go up.

Compare these two scenarios:

Just the facts:

Shopper: How much is your spay?

Receptionist: We charge $120 for a 50-pound dog.

Shopper:	Okay, thanks. 'Bye.

Better:

Shopper:	How much is your spay?
Receptionist:	What kind of dog do you have?... You'll find it's most cost-effective, and best for your dog, to have the spay done before her first heat. Are you familiar with the procedure?... It's performed in our modern surgical suite. Dr. Toney uses the safest anesthetics available. For a 50-pound dog, the total charge is $120. That includes the preoperative physical exam, anesthesia, technician time, surgery, post-surgical monitoring, and the overnight hospital stay. You're welcome to stop by for a tour. When would you like to come in?

According to an article in *Veterinary Economics*, about 65% to 75% of new callers should be scheduling appointments.[1] The article suggests keeping a "new client caller log" for several months to monitor results. If your scheduling rate is close to 75% but not enough people are calling, you need to increase awareness of your practice. On the other hand, if a large percentage of your callers ask about your fees but don't make an appointment, don't assume your prices are too high. The real problem may be that your receptionists don't have time to explain your services fully, or perhaps they immediately classify callers who ask about fees as phone shoppers and dismiss them without further thought.

Dr. Robert Cartin says:

> *People tend to assume that phone shoppers are shopping for the lowest cost, but very often they are not. If you engage them in conversation and ask about the pet, they may not care about the lowest price but that you were nice on the phone. It's not easy to take the time when you're busy, but the clients on the other end couldn't care less—they don't know how busy you are.*

Owl Creek Veterinary Hospital in Virginia Beach, VA, reports getting an average of six new clients a month simply by taking the time to tell people who call what makes Owl Creek special. That's 72 new clients a year just by educating phone shoppers.[2]

Support for the Telephone Receptionist

A policy alone will not relieve your phone problems. Often the problems are a sign of understaffing or inadequate job descriptions, not just the lack of a clear policy.

Although the telephone is just a technological device, in many ways it is the heart of the practice, linking clients to you and saying far more about the practice, staff, and veterinarians than the words that come through the line. When the connection exceeds client expectations, clients gain a professional, personal image of the practice. The telephone often presents the first opportunity to tell a client, "We're knowledgeable. We care about you. You can count on us."

Telephone excellence—attentive, responsive, friendly, and personal service—doesn't happen by accident. It's a team effort, the result of education, motivation, and good management.

Notes

1. D. Tumblin and C. Wutchiett. Slow Growth? Your Fees May Not be the Problem. *Veterinary Economics*, Oct 1996: 54–59.
2. A. Ashby. Grow Your Practice. *AAHA Trends*, May 1995:17–19.

Action Steps for a Great Connection

1. Hire and train telephone receptionists who are mature and intelligent. The person who answers the telephone is the voice of the practice.

2. Establish standards for telephone response, and make sure they are followed.

3. Periodically, have someone conduct a telephone "mystery shopper survey" to monitor how callers are treated.

4. Don't overburden the telephone receptionist with responsibilities. In a busy practice, handling the phones is a demanding job. The telephone receptionist should be able to focus on the caller.

5. Make sure clients know when a return call from the veterinarian can be expected. Develop a phone triage schedule so that staffers know what calls to route and to whom to route them.

6. Consider a telephone company evaluation of your system if clients frequently encounter a busy signal or are put on hold.

Chapter 12

The Waiting Room Dilemma

I couldn't get in to see my vet when my cat was sick, so I went elsewhere—Iowa cat owner[1]

Seen on time? That actually happens? I'd say on average, my vet runs about 30 minutes late. One Saturday I waited an hour. No one informed me about how long I should expect to wait. If I had been told, I could have run an errand and still been back in time. Interestingly, there's a sign posted saying that clients who are more than 30 minutes late may have their appointments rescheduled— Ohio dog owner

Somewhere along the path of progress in veterinary medicine, disregard for client appointment times became institutionalized in the structure of many practices. (Just take a look at the size of some waiting rooms!) Some people have become accustomed to calling the clinic before an appointment to learn "how late the veterinarian is running" so they can plan accordingly.

Does your schedule allow you to run your practice on time? Does a 3 p.m. appointment mean 3:45 on a good day? Do you usually work through your lunch hour, and well past closing time? When you are chronically running late, something is wrong. Are you delegating appropriate tasks to your technician? Are you setting aside enough time in your schedule for each appointment, or are you still pretending (wishing) that appointments that take 20 minutes can be squeezed into a 10-minute slot?

Waiting = Irritability

You may have noticed (if you've made the effort to ask) that your own clients are irritable about spending too much time in your reception area. Good practices with excellent clinicians and fine service and care can lose clients because they don't take this problem seriously enough. Fortunately, it is manageable. We know it is, because we've encountered a number of busy, successful practices in which clients don't wait. These veterinarians and their staffs realize that their clients expect them to honor the schedule, barring emergencies. They have made a commitment to being on time and have found ways to stay on schedule without neglecting in-hospital treatments or shortchanging their clients in the exam room.

Too many veterinarians, however—the same ones who speak with sincerity and enthusiasm of the importance of service—have confessed that their clients wait, sometimes an inordinate amount of time.

Would your clients give you this lackluster "endorsement?"

> There are always new vets with more advanced record keeping and who are more efficient. My vet is okay, but someone could always be better.[2]

Imagine how little it would take for this client to switch to a more efficient practice.

Not a Subject To Be Taken Lightly

Although some veterinarians make light of waiting time, clients, for all their joking, do not treat it lightly. A practice that keeps clients waiting routinely without justification not only incurs client wrath but also penalizes itself. A reception area chock full of clients glancing at their watches is symptomatic of a problem. The problem is inefficiency, and the symptom is poor service. This inefficiency has these harmful effects:

+ People and processes are not as productive as they could be. This means lost income and higher overhead costs.

+ Clients are displeased, and may not return. They definitely won't give you or your practice rave reviews. This translates directly to lost income because most practices depend on client referrals for continued growth.

+ Displeased clients often express their unhappiness to staff members, which creates stress and dissatisfaction in employees. (Don't count on your employees to tell you, unless you've shown you *want* to hear about, and take action on, complaints!)

+ A lengthy wait affects clients' perception of quality.

+ Excessive waiting time conveys a lack of respect for the client's time, as though it's not as important as the doctor's time.

When we asked good veterinarians who said they believe in quality service about waiting time, we heard excuses such as, "Well, we're doing everything else right. Our clients like us and appreciate what we do for them. We have the latest equipment and techniques. So clients really don't mind waiting."

Really? Ask them sometime. New clients unfamiliar with the practice and the veterinarians don't get a favorable impression when the visit starts out with an extended introduction to the reception-area wallpaper pattern. Clients who have been with your practice for some time may tolerate the long wait (changing veterinarians is a major hassle, after all), but it does taint their perception of your quality. It's another negative moment of truth to add to their overall impression of your practice.

Coping on "Those" Days

Even the most efficient practice occasionally (and sometimes frequently) has days when the calendar is crammed, emergencies overrun the normally smooth schedule, clients arrive late with stories of traffic backups, and every client seems to have several complaints in addition to the presenting problem. When the inevitable delays occur and the waiting room is indeed a *waiting* room, some alternative strategies may ease the frustration for clients and help them while away the time.

Like most veterinarians, Dr. Gary Johnson of Dana Niguel Veterinary Hospital in Dana Point, CA, sometimes sees cases that will require more of his time than the 15-minute appointment.

> *It's all very unpredictable. Human medicine is a lot more predictable. In our case, people will call and say "Fifi isn't feeling well," and when they come in, it's a disaster that takes two hours of emergency surgery.*

For instances where a pet's condition is not an emergency but will require more than the allotted 15-minute appointment, Dr. Johnson offers them the option of leaving the pet and calling later for a progress report.

The best service strategy for unexpected delays is to *tell the client.* Call those who may not have left their home or office yet. Clients already waiting appreciate being informed; an explanation or apology from a staff member makes them feel better even though it doesn't change the fact that they must wait. Acknowledgment from the veterinarian helps, too. Several veterinarians told us that they make a point of apologizing if they've kept their clients waiting too long. They also said that many clients are amazed to hear a veterinarian say, "I'm sorry you had to wait." In fact, some pet owners we spoke with said they had *never* had a veterinarian's office call to warn them that they were running late. Imagine the impression you'll make if you do!

Managing Waiting Time

Fortunately, many veterinarians are aware that clients see the minutes stack up and are paying closer attention to their schedules. Perhaps they've received one too many blistering comments from clients who are tired of restructuring their daily schedule following an unplanned chunk of time in their waiting room.

Take waiting time as seriously as your clients do.
Methods you can use to create a smooth-flowing
schedule include:

+ Not taking walk-in appointments

+ Leaving room in the schedule throughout the day
  for emergencies

+ Scheduling time for routine morning and evening
  treatments ("fitting them in" translates to delayed
  or forgotten)

+ Allowing time for surgery, radiography, analyzing
  laboratory results, unexpected in-hospital treatments,
  and other procedures that don't involve contact with
  clients

+ Allotting exam time according to the complaint

+ Communicating to clients the expectation that they
  must be on time

+ Communicating clearly to staff your commitment to
  an on-time schedule, and gaining their cooperation
  and commitment

+ Cross-training all the staff to ensure maximum
  efficiency

+ Delegating appropriate tasks to your technician

"Technicians have the ability to generate more income
by being delegated tasks that the veterinarian used to
do", says registered technician Pat Navarre. "That frees
up the veterinarian to expand the services of the
practice."[3]

Fritz Wood, CPA, recommends that before a veterinarian does anything, he or she should ask, "Can someone
else do it?" That allows the doctor to have more time to
examine more patients every day, and to spend time on
value-added work—work that clients are willing to pay
for and that advances the business financially.[4]

A practice manager for a physician who was consistently
45 minutes to an hour late each day told us how the staff
cured the problem. After pleading and pointing out how
angry waiting patients became, the manager left the first
hour unscheduled for several days. When the physician

Table 12.1 Scheduling Options

Type of Schedule	Advantages	Disadvantages
Stream	Easy; standard books available	Inflexible; excessive client waiting time; idle time for doctor and staff
Wave	Reduces idle time for doctor, staff	Excessive client waiting time; crowded waiting room
Modified Wave	Reduces idle time for doctor, staff	Possible client backlogs

arrived, late as usual, and learned that no patients were waiting to see her, she was at first livid, but the next day and thereafter she arrived on time. (We don't necessarily endorse this procedure; not all employers are likely to be as understanding or to change their behaviors as easily.)

Scheduling for Client Satisfaction

A smoothly flowing schedule that minimizes waiting time is a significant ingredient in your recipe for client satisfaction and success of your practice. You can accomplish this by creating a practice schedule that's personalized to your style, your staff, and your clients. Let's look first at the most widely used scheduling methods (Table 12.1), each of which has advantages as well as disadvantages. Then we'll go step by step through a process to choose options that will create a customized scheduling method that will work for your practice. There are as many approaches to efficient scheduling as there are styles of practice. And that's the key: A rigid schedule is meaningless and ineffective if it does not take into account the veterinarian's individual style.

The Stream Method

With stream scheduling, one appointment is scheduled after another in a sequence of uniform blocks throughout the day. For example, one client is scheduled at 9 a.m., the next at 9:15, and the third at 9:30. The advantage is that it's easy. Most appointment books are organized for this method. Sream scheduling doesn't work, though, unless all clients require exactly the same amount of time. Clients who are late or don't show up can cause wasted time. On the other hand, a client who needs a longer procedure and extra time for conversation can throw the whole day off schedule.

The Wave or Block Schedule

Using the wave or block system, a specified number of clients are scheduled at one time, and then none are scheduled in subsequent time slots. Six clients may be scheduled at 9 a.m. and the next six at 10 a.m., for example. Wave scheduling eliminates down time for the veterinarian and staff. Even if some clients are late or don't show up, someone is always waiting for the doctor. Clients don't tend to be pleased with this system, however. When several people arrive together, those who wait longer are likely to become upset. Also, after established clients figure out this scheduling system, they learn to manipulate it. Knowing that several appointments are made for the same time and that the person who arrives earliest is seen first, they may arrive a half hour or more ahead of their scheduled appointment just to be sure they're seen first. What an inefficient scheduling system! Imagine what clients must say about this practice as they're whiling away their valuable time in the waiting room.

The Modified Wave Schedule

With the modified wave schedule, a cluster of clients is scheduled at the beginning of each hour, and then individual appointments are scheduled later during the hour. For example, three clients are scheduled at 9 a.m., one at 9:30, and one at 9:45. An alternative modified wave method books two clients at the same time, at the beginning of a time slot long enough to see two clients—for example, two clients at 11 a.m. and two at 11:30.

This method increases the likelihood that a client always will be available when the veterinarian is ready. It can work if auxiliary personnel use the waiting time for the second and third clients to complete paperwork and to do preliminary procedures. If the time required doesn't match up with the time available, however, clients can get backlogged. Also, some clients might wind up waiting 20 or 30 minutes, which is longer than they're likely to tolerate without becoming irritated.

Customized Scheduling

The best solution is to create a customized scheduling system. Its success depends on gathering key information about the characteristics and style of your practice. The first step is to be sure you understand your preferences, your style, and the needs of your staff and clients. Enlist the help and ideas of the entire staff in your evaluation. Answer the following questions, and think about other preferences that should be reflected in your scheduling procedures:

✦ What types of clients do you see? Clients in various age groups and with certain demographic characteristics have different demands on their time that affect when they are able to schedule appointments. (Your client survey—see Chapter 3—will have shown you the most requested days and times.)

✦ How much time should be devoted to new clients? Annual exams? Routine booster vaccinations? Sick animals?

✦ What tasks can be delegated to staff members so you can use your time more efficiently: client education? TPR and history-taking? phone calls? recording client information?

✦ What time should morning and afternoon sessions start and end?

In answering these questions, you can start by doing the following:

✦ Make a commitment to be at the clinic and ready to see clients at the agreed-upon starting time. Clients should not be scheduled significantly before your arrival.

✦ Be sure that your assistant or technician has enough time to complete morning treatments before he or she is needed to help you. That may mean bringing in extra help in the mornings or having the assistant arrive at the clinic an hour before appointments begin.

✦ Schedule extra help on surgery mornings to handle drop-offs, and on those afternoons for pick-ups.

Conducting a Time Audit

The next step in tackling your schedule is to find out what's really going on in your practice. These notes can be used to analyze bottlenecks within the practice and to adjust the schedule accordingly.

1. For two weeks, attach a time audit-form (see Figure 12.1) to each pet's chart. List the client's name and the reason for the visit, and fill in times as the pet moves through the visit, surgery or treatment, or as laboratory samples are drawn and analyzed. Fill in the actual time required to perform each step, not counting the time the client is waiting while you're not working on his or her pet (you're doing something else, then—and recording that, too).

2. Keep time charts to record time not dedicated to one client—time on the phone, in the laboratory, or performing any other procedures that are a regular part of your day.

3. Organize your information. Group into stacks the time-audit forms for similar procedures and examinations into stacks. For each stack add the "total time in clinic" numbers. Then divide this sum by the number of forms in the stack. This is the average time required for each category. Look back through your appointment book to see whether any procedures were missed in your audit. List them with the approximate time required. Have your technician do the same.

4. Classify each day as busy, average, or quiet. Analyze daily and weekly patterns of visits. Are Mondays busy? Do Thursday afternoons tend to be quiet? What is your pattern of urgent appointments, walk-ins, and routine visits?

The time audit will reveal each veterinarian's personal style of practice. If clients typically are allotted a 15-

Figure 12.1 Time Audit Chart

Date/Day of week _____   Client _____

Reason for visit _____

Procedure	Receptionist Time in/out		Technician Time in/out		Veterinarian Time in/out	
Arrival						
Check-in						
Exam room						
Treatment						
Outpatient						
In-hospital						
Laboratory						
Taking samples						
Analyzing samples						
Radiology						
Taking radiographs						
Analyzing radiographs						
Surgery prep						
Surgery						
Surgical recovery						

minute interval and you're spending an average of 25 minutes per client, adjustments are indicated. More time should be given to each appointment, or you need to change your style (not realistic if you've been practicing for any length of time).

Another option is to use staff members to perform routine tasks that hinder your productivity—but leave yourself enough time during the appointment to build rapport with clients. Many practices pair each doctor with a specific technician for the day so that technician is available for assistance when needed.

Creating Scheduling Protocols

Now you're ready to develop written scheduling protocols that reflect the preferences and patterns of your practice. A staff member should be asked to take the information gathered during the time audit and make a list of the most common procedures performed in your practice. This can be used to create an easy-to-use chart listing the time needed for each kind of visit. When Ms. Gage calls to make an appointment for a recheck of her dog's tibial fracture, for instance, the dog may need 20 minutes with the technician in radiology and 15 minutes with the doctor in the exam room. Allowing adequate time for tasks increases efficiency and decreases wasted time.

After the duration of appointments has been determined, a staff meeting should be held with front and back personnel and the veterinarians to discuss this and the issues listed next, as well as any other concerns unique to your situation. The most important thing is to identify your needs, set reasonable protocols, and then stick to them!

Setting Saturday Hours

Evening and Saturday morning appointments are popular with clients. Many clinics that decide to offer Saturday morning appointments find that this turns out to be their busiest time. Yet those practices usually work with half the normal staff and fewer doctors because "it's the weekend." Practices should reevaluate their busy and quiet times and work with everyone to be sure staffing is adequate during rush times.

Consider offering early morning and/or evening hours once or twice a week. Whether you're adding evening or weekend hours, the total number of hours each staff member works could remain the same. Some doctors and staff members can arrive and leave earlier or later. Others may prefer to have one of their days off on a weekday so they can avoid the crowds while running errands.

Survey your clients to learn whether they have an interest in nontraditional hours, or simply try it for a month or two. If you do this, be sure that clients know these appointment times are available. They aren't likely to ask for evenings or noon-time appointments if you've never offered that availability previously.

An AAHA survey showed that 71% of pet owners took advantage of extended hours; about one-third of those took advantage of those hours for every visit, and the rest used the extended hours only occasionally.[5] Expanded hours needn't dig deeply into your time. Clients don't want to come in at 5 a.m. or 10 p.m. unless they have an emergency.

Veterinary Economics surveyed clients about the best times for appointments.[6] In order of preference, the most-desired time periods were:

✦ Saturdays 8 a.m. to 12 p.m.

✦ Weekdays 8 a.m. to 11 a.m.

✦ Weekdays 5 p.m. to 8 p.m.

✦ Weekdays 1 p.m. to 5 p.m.

✦ Saturdays 12 p.m. to 5 p.m.

Why not survey your own clients to find out the times they like best? You may find that taking two afternoons off per week actually fits in quite well with your clients' wishes. You could make up for that time by being open two evenings per week, for example. Why box yourself in to an 8-to-5 job when you can work the same number of hours scattered over your own customized schedule?

Designing a Customized Appointment Book

You now have the means to create an appointment book tailor-made for your practice. Here's how to design a book that works for you.

First look back at your scheduling protocol. What is your mix of lengths for each visit? You likely have a range from 5 minutes to an hour. Next, review your written scheduling protocols. Keeping those in mind, sketch out an ideal appointment book.

Some veterinarians use books with 10-minute appointment slots and multiples of 10 minutes for each type of appointment. The veterinarians and the technicians both may schedule in this way. For instance, a puppy returning for the second of two deworming treatments may require only one 10-minute technician slot, whereas a geriatric cat exam could take three slots of a veterinarian's time.

If that doesn't work for you, simply design your own book. For instance, all veterinarian appointments at Animal Health Centre in Fresno, CA, are 30 minutes long. Dr. Lee Ann DuMars, hospital director, says longer appointments allow the doctor to give personal attention to each pet owner. A technician is always in the room to hold the animal, freeing the client from distraction and keeping the pet under control. "I charge more for an office call than most veterinarians in town," says Dr. DuMars, "but no one has ever complained. They see how thorough I am."[7]

Combining the modified wave schedule with appointment lengths customized to your needs is the best solution for many practices. Alternating long and short blocks can help keep you on schedule.

Look at your busy/average/quiet pattern. Schedule longer visits and routine follow-up appointments during times that are less busy. Maintain a few open slots for urgent visits and referrals, even on busy days.

Keep slots available for new clients. They don't want to wait long for an appointment. If the wait is too long, they'll find another veterinarian because they have formed no bond with your practice. Allow time for telephone calls, hospital consults, meetings, lunch commitments, and so forth. Maintain a waiting list of clients who would prefer an earlier appointment or who are available for cancellation slots.

Include sufficient space in each block to record client name, pet name, day and evening phone numbers, and the reason for the appointment (this is essential to allot enough time, to assign the appropriate exam room, and to assemble equipment). Include any other information that would help you.

Pay attention not only to the daily schedule but also to your weekly and monthly plan. Group practices have a great deal of flexibility in scheduling doctors' and technicians' time. For instance, one three-doctor clinic in Montana is open Monday through Friday, plus Saturday mornings, and is available for 24-hour emergencies. Each doctor and each technician rotates through this schedule: work (and take all emergency calls) all 7 days for one week; work Monday through Thursday the next week, with a 3-day weekend off; and work Monday through Saturday the third week, with Sunday off. That schedule ensures that two doctors are available for Saturday appointments, that one doctor is always available for emergencies, and that each doctor still gets time off.

A two-doctor practice in New Mexico assigns one doctor to work in the back and one to work appointments each day. The doctor in the back examines all in-hospital animals, performs all surgeries, and supervises all in-hospital procedures done that day. The second doctor is thus free to concentrate on appointments and to keep the schedule running smoothly. If a pet shows up for an appointment that requires more time than the schedule has allowed, that pet is "transferred" to the back, where the second veterinarian takes over its care, allowing the first doctor to proceed with waiting clients.

Scheduling Appointments

Clients need to know that you value their calls. The staff should offer alternative times and days in a friendly, accommodating way, balancing client convenience with your need to fill appointment slots efficiently. The scheduler should be well trained to screen clients effectively. To ensure that the proper amount of time is allocated, clients should be asked these questions:

✦ What is the reason for your visit? What signs has your pet been showing? For how long?

✦ Have we seen this pet here before?

✦ If yes, have we seen the pet for this problem before?

✦ How are your other pets doing? Will you bring any of them in at the same time?

✦ If the visit is for a routine vaccination, ask specifically whether the client has any other questions about the pet's health that should be addressed during the visit.

Switching from Drop-Ins to Scheduling Appointments

When my partners and I bought this practice 11 years ago, it was a hospital that grossed about $1 million, and everything came in on a walk-in basis. It was very chaotic, but busy. If you had asked us what we thought good service was, we would have said that it meant being able to come in any time. What we found, though, is that we had to spend an awful lot of time justifying fees, handling complaints, and dealing with things that we no longer spend a lot of time on. One of the major problems was that chaos. It might have been convenient to walk in, but it wasn't convenient once the client got here.

We decided to make an enormous shift. People were comfortable with the walk-in schedule, but if you really asked them, their answer would indicate that if you could make it convenient and still have appointments, it would be a lot nicer when they came in. We began by asking our clients if they were willing to come in at a specific time of day. We had a transitional period with lots of walk-ins and appointments. With only two exam rooms, it was difficult juggling the work. Now we see many more people than we did back then, and it seems calm.

Dr. Thomas Austin's experience at Newport Harbor Animal Hospital may sound like your own. Are you continuing with a walk-in protocol just because that's the way you've always done it or because you're afraid of how your clients will respond to change? Think of the benefits that will result from establishing an appointment schedule, then educate your clients of the benefits to *them*.

Staying on Schedule

After you have developed a schedule that works for your practice, stay on schedule with these tips:

✦ Book designated phone time into the schedule. Squeezing in calls or interrupting examinations is not wise. Many practices find that 20-minute blocks in the morning and afternoon streamline callbacks.

✦ Authorize staff members to let veterinarians know when they are running behind schedule. Dr. Robert Cartin plans to have his staff members start a timer at the moment they put out a client's chart so the doctors know how long the client has been waiting.

✦ To speed the flow, change the order in which you see clients. See a quick client ahead of one you know will require more time.

✦ Take time to talk to clients, recognizing that some clients need extra time and attention. At times, though, clients' needs extend well beyond the stated reason for the visit. If a client makes an appointment for one problem and then brings up several others during the examination or brings other pets to be seen, schedule a separate appointment, explaining that the problems deserve appropriate time and attention. Some veterinarians give the client a choice of dropping off the pet for later treatment or bringing it in at another time.

Reducing No-Shows

Clients who don't show up for appointments are a major drain on efficiency. (This also may reflect dissatisfaction and pose a liability risk, so keeping track of no-shows and following up with them is a good idea.) The most common reasons people become no-shows are that:

✦ They are afraid of the procedure or diagnosis, or they don't understand the reason for or importance of the appointment.

✦ The appointment time is not convenient, or they are annoyed at long waiting times during previous visits.

✦ They've neglected to record the appointment date and time and simply forgot it.

✦ Your policy is to ask for payment at the time of the visit, and they don't have the money.

✦ They felt pressured to make the appointment and didn't know how to say so. Instead of figuring out how to address their discomfort, they simply sidestep the issue. (Are you offering, or are you pushing? Educating, or "telling" pet owners about the need for the appointment?)

How To Reduce No-shows

✦ To create an affiliation with the practice, send a welcome letter and information about the practice in advance of new clients' appointments.

✦ Call clients the day before the appointment to confirm.

✦ Call no-show clients to ask why they didn't show up and to reschedule their appointments. Keep a "no-show notebook" with client name, day and evening phone numbers, time and date of broken appointment, reason for visit, and response. If the client does not reschedule, the veterinarian may want to follow up.

✦ Document all no-shows, and the practice's attempts to contact them, for medical and legal reasons. If a no-show is a referral, send a written notice to the referring veterinarian.

✦ Give follow-up clients a reminder card to take home. The card should indicate your cancellation policy: "If you must cancel, please call 555-0000, 24 hours in advance, so we may give your time slot to another client and make another appointment for you."

✦ Give clients whose pets need a return visit a "treatment plan." Note the date and time of the next appointment, why the patient is coming back, what is planned, and how the client can participate in the pet's care. Because informed clients will be more likely to understand the importance of the next appointment, they are more likely to be there.

✦ Send out yearly exam reminder cards 2-3 weeks before the exam is due. Many veterinarians now stress the physical exam, not just vaccinations, in this reminder. Call clients who have not responded within one week of their due date; they may have misplaced the reminder.

Keep these issues in mind when dealing with clients, and try to communicate your concern and willingness to discuss and solve problems. Following the suggestions in this chapter will put the satisfaction of everyone—veterinarians, staff, and clients—on schedule.

Notes

1. American Animal Hospital Association. *1995 AAHA Report: A Study of the Companion Animal Veterinary Services Market: 106–110.*
2. *1995 AAHA Report.*
3. M. Osika. The Secret of Your Success: Your Technician. AAHA *Trends,* Aug/Sep 1992: 41–42.

Action Steps for a Satisfying Schedule

1. Do a time audit to monitor client waiting time in the reception area and in the exam room.

2. Analyze the veterinarian's style. Accommodate the schedule to veterinarian style.

3. Analyze the types of problems you see and the time they take. Adapt appointments accordingly.

4. Delegate tasks to use veterinarian time efficiently and effectively.

5. Convene the staff to identify problems and discuss realistic solutions.

6. Be sure that everyone participates in and understands the rationale for and objectives of changes. When people invest in new ideas, they are more motivated to make the system work.

7. If you are pinpointed as part of the waiting time bottleneck, listen with an open mind.

8. Monitor and nurture your new system, and make adjustments as necessary.

4. F. Wood. Top Consultants Spot Problems and Opportunities. In *Mastering the Marketplace: Taking Your Practice to the Top* (Ross Clark, ed). Lenexa, KS: Veterinary Medicine Publishing, 1996: 43
5. *1995 AAHA Report.*
6. W. Myers. What Do Clients Want? *Veterinary Economics*, June 1997:40–49.
7. R. Hawn. *AAHA Trends*, Dec/Jan 1997: 24–25.

Chapter 13

A Partnership with Clients

I'm here to listen—and help. Not: Let me tell you.....—Tom Peters [1]

Unable to tolerate his cat's constant sneezing, his own nagging worry, or his worried spouse any longer, Mr. Roth has decided to take the cat to a veterinarian. Asking around, he gets a favorable recommendation from two coworkers. He calls your clinic, has a positive interaction with your telephone receptionist, and is able to make an appointment at a convenient time.

Now he is ready to meet you and your staff for diagnosis, discussion, and treatment. His perception of this brief time spent with you and your staff depends on everything he sees, hears, and senses in the practice: what the practice itself looks like, how he is greeted, and the professionalism of the technician who weighs the cat and takes his temperature.

Once you enter the exam room, it's pretty much up to you. Mr. Roth will listen, observe, and evaluate. Like it or not, much of the cat's medical outcome depends on the rapport—the partnership—that develops between the two of you. If Mr. Roth is comfortable with that partnership, he's more likely to listen carefully to you, to ask questions, to follow your advice, and to do his part of the work necessary to keep his cat healthy. If he believes you're concerned about him and his cat, not just his cat's sneezing, Mr. Roth is likely to regard your veterinary care as high-quality. On the other hand, if your rapport is limited, he is likely to evaluate the veterinary care as poor.

How do you make the client feel that he or she has your undivided, caring attention, especially in the typically hectic practice? Treat your clients and their pets as individuals. Show personal interest and concern. Look at the pet and its owner as a whole—not just a problem or a disease.

Creating Rapport

Establishing rapport in a brief visit takes plain old "people skills." These come more naturally to some people than to others. Here are a few tips:

✦ Familiarize yourself with the pet's history before you enter the exam room. Don't read the chart and ask questions at the same time; clients need your attention and eye contact. You may be impressed by your abilities to read, write, and ask questions all at the same time, but your clients won't.

✦ If you've asked clients to fill out a veterinary history, particularly a lengthy one, take the time to read their answers. Clients say they don't mind filling out questionnaires if they think the information is used, but they resent filling them out and then being asked the same questions verbally with no indication that their written responses were reviewed.

✦ Extend your hand to each client for an adult-to-adult handshake. If an interpreter is needed for someone whose language you don't speak or for someone who is deaf or hearing impaired, make eye contact with the client, not the interpreter or signer, when you reply.

✦ Wash your hands in the exam room in front of the client. Clients appreciate your attention to basic hygiene.

✦ Ask a personal question first. Ask about the client's job, children, or other pets. Beginning with social conversation can quickly establish empathy and personal interest. Some veterinarians make notes in the client's veterinary record to remind them of nonveterinary subjects—a daughter graduating from college, a new job started last month, an award. (Keep it brief, though; rambling on about nonveterinary subjects ruins your schedule and annoys some clients.)

✦ Make the client's priorities your priorities. Ask, "What's new in your life right now?" The answer may lead you to a better diagnosis. Consider the woman whose asthmatic cat has suddenly worsened. She answers your query with, "My daughter has moved back into the house, and her smoking drives me nuts!"

✦ Make a note in the pet's chart for problems to follow up on. If today's appointment is for an ear problem but the pet was in for an abscess 3 months ago, ask about the abscess.

✦ Convey to clients early in your relationship that medicine isn't an exact science. Establish an open, honest, adult-to-adult relationship. Let them know that you're in this together and that an effective veterinarian-client relationship will have its share of ups and downs.

Emphasizing Communication

> My cat was once ill with constipation and had not had a bowel movement for a few days. I took her to the vet and he just literally blew up at me. He yelled at me like I was a stupid idiot and didn't care at all about the life of my cat (which couldn't be further from the truth). He said she had 14 inches of feces built up (does that sound possible?) in her intestines and could have easily died. I was, to say the least, shocked at his treatment of me. I obviously wouldn't be spending the money for vet care if I didn't care about my cat. I didn't appreciate being yelled at and berated by my vet. I felt bad enough without him doing that. —Indiana cat owner

Clear communication is the backbone of building rapport. Too little, the wrong kind, or communication without empathy has been pinpointed as the impetus for malpractice suits that may have been avoided.

What Is Good Communication?

Research as found that clients are most satisfied with communication that encompasses the following characteristics:

✦ Information

✦ Technical and interpersonal competence

✦ Partnership building

✦ Social conversation

✦ Positive rather than negative talk

✦ Longer duration (Duration is a matter of perception. Communication that takes place as part of a satisfying interaction will be perceived favorably no matter now long or short the actual time span.

Source: Meta-analysis of Correlates of Provider Behaviors in Medical Encounters, by J. A. Hall, D. L. Roter, and D. R. Katz, in Medical Care, 26(1988): 657–675.

The connection created between veterinarian and client is the thread that weaves client satisfaction and a successful practice together. It's what makes clients loyal, makes them follow instructions, pay their bills on time, forgive mistakes, feel confident about your competence, and send friends to your practice. The rapport you create with your clients brings them back. Effective, interactive communication is healthy for clients because it gives them a sense of control in what can be an otherwise intimidating experience.

When concluding a client visit, say, "Let's be sure we agree on our plan." Getting your client to participate and believe in your treatment plan by explaining options and alternatives and the merits and negatives of each aids compliance and assures you that the client understands what to expect.

Some clients don't follow instructions because they think it's not important to do so, or they don't comprehend what will happen if they don't fill the prescription, feed fewer treats to help reduce their pets' weight, come in for a follow-up appointment, or stick to the recommended pet food. Or they don't understand what a high-fiber diet is, or why the full 10 days of antibiotics must be administered, or the risk of not keeping the bandage dry. Or they can't figure out how to get the pill down their cat's throat.

What we have in all of these instances is a failure to communicate. Compliance depends on thorough, complete communication.

Avoid using veterinary jargon. Think of how you might describe a condition or treatment to an eighth-grade child, and speak so that he or she could understand you. Say "blood in the urine" rather than "hematuria," "fluid in the joint" rather than "joint effusion."

When seeing clients, consider having an assistant or a veterinary technician with you. Some veterinarians use the staffer as a record keeper, a scribe who takes notes as the veterinarian and client talk. The staff member also restrains the pet. This keeps the veterinarian's and the client's attention on why they are there. The technician also can watch the client for signs of attention and understanding and help explain any scientific jargon you inadvertently let slip out.

With good rapport, your client feels comfortable telling you she won't be able to get the medicine into her dog's ear (rather than nodding and going home to a losing battle). These problems frequently can be resolved by offering to hospitalize a pet that is difficult to medicate. The dog with a painful, inflamed ear may become more comfortable after a few days of in-hospital treatment and then will allow the owner to administer further treatments at home.

Conclude your clinical visit in the exam room. Don't continue your conversation in the public hallway or at the checkout desk. It's too easy to say things such as, "Now if your dog continues to mount your leg, we can try some other approaches." Clients may seem cordial during an exchange like this, but they're probably plotting secretly how to humiliate *you* in front of your employees.

Learning to Listen

For some veterinarians, communication means talk. In the belief that clients consult them for their wisdom and that wisdom is evidenced by sage advice and extensive use of veterinary terminology, these veterinarians talk—a lot.

All this talk gets results, but not necessarily the desired results. The ratio of veterinarian chatter to client satisfaction is inversely proportional: The more the veterinarian talks compared to the client, the less satisfied the client will be.

Many veterinarians focus solely on what they are saying without paying attention to the receiver or the results (did the client not only hear the message but also understand it correctly?). Concerned about time, veterinarians hesitate to use open-ended questions or statements ("Tell me what you're concerned about, Mr. Phelps.") for fear that they will open the verbal flood-gates.

Veterinarians can learn from the research done with physicians. Sociolinguist Richard Frankel, MD, of the University of Rochester Medical School reviewed medical interviews between internists and their patients and found that 51 of 74 physicians interrupted their patients within 18 seconds of the patient's explanation.[2] Another study found that physicians spend less than 2 minutes of a 20-minute visit actually providing information.[3]

When you conduct the veterinary interview in the traditional veterinarian-centered way, you may believe that quality veterinary care has taken place. You've made a diagnosis, prescribed a treatment, shook Ms. Crane's hand, and wished her a good day as you left the exam room. You've fulfilled your technical role, but was the veterinarian-client relationship enhanced? You may be satisfied—you've accomplished your objective of dispensing veterinary care—but your client is not. The building blocks of the relationship are stacked in place, but the glue of effective two-way communication is missing. Without it, so are the results you seek: client compliance, a better outcome, and, most of all, client satisfaction.

Enhancing Interaction

Enough negative talk! The question is: What can you do to improve communication and client satisfaction?

After all, clients do need to hear your diagnosis, your instructions, and your advice. Your clients come to you for your wisdom and veterinary expertise. First, however, they must have *their* chance to talk. If given the opportunity to talk freely, clients actually will take less time to summarize their complaint.

In truth, an uninterrupted narrative usually takes about 1 or 2 minutes on average, or about 2.5 minutes at most. During this narrative the veterinarian's role should be to engage in active listening. That means taking your hand off the doorknob and giving your client your full attention.

An active listener responds: "And what did that cough sound like?" or "What I hear you saying is…" Active listening lets your client know that you have heard what he or she has said. It shows concern and interest. It positions the veterinarian as both veterinary expert and interpersonal communicator—roles to which clients give equal value.

A satisfying interaction is one in which the client gets the chance to tell you the facts about the pet's signs *and* his or her opinion of where the problem lies. An affiliative veterinarian is one whose communication style establishes a positive relationship with clients through friendliness, interest, empathy, a nonjudgmental attitude, and a social orientation.[4] That's the style of house-call veterinarian Dr. Nancy Murbach, who has found that a personal touch helps work through diagnostic dilemmas:

> One of my clients had an Amazon parrot with a feather-picking/self-mutilation problem that had just begun. I asked all the usual questions, with no answers coming out. Finally she sighed and said that with her daughter's pending divorce and her move back home, it was a wonder she herself wasn't pulling out her hair. I jumped on it and asked for more information.
>
> It turned out the daughter was constantly in a rage and couldn't have a normal conversation with her mother, and [the client] had noticed that the bird seemed agitated and yelled whenever the daughter

did. She just hadn't realized how that could affect the bird. If she hadn't gotten to the point of sharing that little tidbit, who knows? She told the daughter in no uncertain terms that she either had to behave civilly or move out—doctor's orders!

Using Restraint in Communication

In addition to the typical "yes–no" questions, use open-ended questions. For example, before asking, "Does Frankie seem to get tired after exercise?" say, "Tell me how Frankie is doing these days, Ms. Crane." She may describe her frustration at Frankie's not liking to go on long walks the way he used to. Open-ended questions elicit information and revelations that don't come out of "yes–no" questions. They also are interactive, nurturing the doctor-client relationship.

Listen. Bite your tongue, put your hand over your mouth, do whatever it takes to stay silent until Ms. Crane is through speaking. Most clients will synopsize the problem and complete their explanation within a few minutes. You have to give clients a chance to tell their story, even if it's unrelated to their veterinary-complaint. Until they do, they're not ready to hear what you have to say, no matter how important it may be. If someone does begin to ramble, you can bring him or her back gently by saying, "I'd like to focus on the vomiting you just mentioned."

Don't give in to the urge to dive into a break in the conversational flow. Not only is silence golden, it can be productive. When your client is fumbling for words, he or she may be overcoming nervousness or formulating a difficult statement. Give him or her the space and time to verbalize it. Nonjudgmental comments ("I'm worried about Frankie's weight") and appropriate "uhhuhs" and "hmms" are simple ways to demonstrate verbally that you're listening and to convey the concern and interest you feel.

Paraphrase the client's complaint, restating it as you heard it. You might say, "Ms. Crane, what I hear you say is that you're concerned about Frankie's lack of energy and especially the fact he is getting so finicky about his food. And since he's getting old, you're afraid these symptoms might be indicative of something more serious. Is that right?" Paraphrasing shows active listening on your part while allowing you to probe for the meaning in your client's statements. It also allows your client to confirm, correct, or add to what you heard.

Using Language That Gets Results

I hate being told what to do. If you ask me to do something, I'll usually say yes. But don't tell me what to do.

You may have friends with a similar attitude. And some of your clients do, too! Learn to change your language patterns to get people to understand and agree with you. These word patterns will also help you get more from your staff.[5]

✦ Instead of saying "You have to," ask "Will you?"

✦ Replace "I'll try" with "I will."

✦ Instead of "No," say "You can" or "You have several choices."

✦ Replace "I can't…" with "The technician/doctor/ practice manager can…"

To increase rapport, professionals have to keep in mind that their priorities are not the same as their clients'. Although you think pets should be spayed or neutered to control overpopulation, your clients are more likely to comply with your advice if you tell them that females will have a lower risk of breast cancer and males a lower risk of prostate problems or anal tumors if they undergo the surgery. (We know it's "mammary cancer" and "perianal adenocarcinoma," but does your client?) One veterinarian's approach to people who are hesitant to neuter male dogs is to say, "Since you aren't planning to neuter Buster, I will show you how to examine the testicles and anal area for evidence of tumors. It's important to monitor these areas in intact dogs." She reports a much higher rate of neutering as a result.

More Than Just Words

Effective communication in the veterinarian-client encounter is two-way and free-flowing. This can be difficult for veterinarians who were taught the traditional veterinary approach that calls for control, power, and authority. The traditional approach is veterinarian-focused. It says to the client, "Listen to my questions, give me the answers I want, and wait for my authorization to speak."

The paternalistic "doctor knows best" model in medicine has a rich and lengthy history. Small wonder, then, that some veterinarians have a hard time with clients who question the doctors' decisions or demand to see X-rays, lab reports, and test results. It's not their style, and it's certainly not veterinary tradition to share information fully with clients or to seek their opinions. If you see a little bit of yourself in that description, consider changing your approach. Effective communication requires establishing a partnership between you and your clients.

Creating an Informed Partnership

A partner is a person associated with another in some activity of common interest. A partnership implies a relationship in which each has equal status and a certain independence but also implicit or formal obligations to the other. The partnership concept is difficult for some veterinarians to accept. It may seem that clients want to dictate to them, prescribing treatment, medication, and follow-up (after they've consulted a lay veterinary care network of family and friends, read the latest promotional flyer they got from the breeder, and self-diagnosed their pet's illness). The print media play its part, too. Pick up any popular magazine or book list and you'll come across articles such as "How To Be Your Own Veterinarian" and "Herbs You Can Use to Treat Your Dog."

Are clients taking control, or are they simply asserting their rights? What should the veterinarian-client relationship look, sound, and feel like? How should it work?

The evidence, plus responses from pet owners and veterinarians we interviewed, suggests that most clients prefer to defer to the veterinarian when it comes to the ultimate recommendation. What they want is information and discussion before making the decision. Most people want to know the pros and cons, and they want the chance to weigh them.

The amount and apparent depth of information you offer, and your honesty, are likely to influence your clients' perception of the quality of the service they receive. You act as a partner in helping them reach a decision, making recommendations based on your knowledge. The help you provide makes their decision easier because it's based on information. If you take over the decision-making without offering information or data to support it, your clients are likely to feel pressured, resentful, patronized, and to resist your suggestions.

Pet owners seek an informed partnership that's grounded in trust and built on facts and judgment, a partnership in which significant decisions or recommendations reside with the most knowledgeable party. In the veterinary encounter, that's you.

Even in a partnership, the person with greater knowledge and expertise must sometimes take over. In an emergency or in the case of a severe illness, people turn to someone who is credible, someone in authority. When clients demand something that is not appropriate, the doctor must be comfortable in saying, "I don't recommend that." If the client isn't convinced, the veterinarian may not have established a strong relationship with the client to begin with.

Collaboration that results from education is the most effective and productive decision-making process (see Chapter 4). If you give clients information, most of them are capable of making their own decisions, and they appreciate the respect it shows you have for them.

Appreciating the Partnership Style

"Partnership" doesn't mean that only one style is acceptable. An article in the *Journal of the American Medical Association* described four models of the physician-client relationship,[6] which easily apply to the veterinarian-client relationship. Each relationship depends on the veterinarian's understanding of the client's values.

1. The *informative model,* in which the client is given all relevant facts to make a decision; the veterinarian's role is that of "technical expert."

2. The *interpretive model,* which is more collaborative; the veterinarian helps the client by providing facts, risks, and benefits and then aids in determining an appropriate course of action.

3. The *deliberative model,* which requires the veterinarian to act as friend or teacher, providing information, and then, through dialogue with the client, recommending a course of action.

4. The *paternalistic model,* also referred to as the *parental model,* in which the veterinarian acts as guardian to the client, sharing selected information and encouraging a course of action for the client's well-being.

The authors point out that there may be an appropriate time and place for each model. An emergency may demand quick action without client consent, for example, calling for the paternalistic model. Overall, though, they believe the deliberative model is the ideal relationship.

Encouraging Client Involvement

Quality care requires clients to speak up for themselves. They must realize that if their pets are having problems at night, the veterinarian should be informed. Yet, clients often are concerned about taking too much of your time. They have concerns but won't express them, or they don't always hear what you have to say, out of concern that they are usurping more than their fair share of your busy schedule.

The burden is on veterinarians to break down barriers with clients who are not forthcoming. You need to help clients become actively involved in the partnership, and to make them feel comfortable in doing so. (Chapter 4 offers more help in educating your clients.)

Some of your clients may have unrealistic expectations of absolute cure or of no risk or complications from veterinary procedures. Others may think that the more technology that is used, the better the result. Superior

How To Get Your Clients Involved

Foster proactive clients by:

+ Giving them information and emphasizing the importance of reviewing and understanding it so they become knowledgeable about their pet's health, illness, symptoms, medications, and treatment.

+ Asking for feedback and responding to it ("Are we meeting your needs? Do you have any questions?").

+ Encouraging them to bring along a family member to support them and to speak up if necessary.

+ Posing questions yourself to let them know you want to hear *their* questions ("You may wonder why I chose this particular vaccine. Let me explain...").

+ Letting them know that you expect them to ask questions.

+ Complimenting them for being responsible pet owners.

customer service includes educating these clients about realistic goals and expectations for their pets.

Client participation is especially important in managing chronic diseases. When the disease is a daily part of their pets' lives, clients must take long-term responsibility for sticking to the treatment or management plan. Drug therapy, a special diet, and exercise programs are all elements of the treatment plan that require understanding and agreement. An informed and educated client is more likely to comply.

Most veterinarians agree that if clients have participated in decisions relating to a specific regimen, they will be more likely to carry it out. You and your staff play an important role as educators, negotiators, motivators, and coaches. Veterinarians and practice staff can influence a client's willingness to stick to a care plan. You also can change your clients' perceptions and self-confidence regarding their ability to influence their pet's health through their own actions.

Dr. Robert Cartin uses this approach:

> I always try to say, "If this were my dog, this is what I would do." If they can't afford the best

option, we try to work with them. We try not to make pet owners feel guilty.

Your staff has a pivotal role. If your staff members are well acquainted with your typical treatment plans, they can reinforce and provide greater detail for your instructions. After you have left the exam room, your technician or assistant should ask the client if he or she understood everything you reviewed. Often, a client is less hesitant to admit uncertainty to a technician than to the veterinarian. Thus, your staff members can offer a safety valve by double-checking whether the client heard your instructions accurately—or by determining whether you heard your client's perceptions and fears accurately.

Good Intentions, But...

Clients are not programmable; they are people who stuff an assortment of personal or social problems and perspectives into their bags of good intentions. All the following can impair or prevent adherence to treatment plans: lack of adequate finances, physical inability to administer medication, a pet's aggressive or unruly behavior that prevents medicating, time or transportation problems, family pressures, religious beliefs, outside opinions, work obligations, and lack of connection or relationship with the veterinarian. Yet, if the veterinarian or a staff member listens to Mr. Keyes and explains why he must give Blue, his Persian kitten, all of her antibiotic rather than save half of it "for the next time she gets a cold," the impact of these factors can be mitigated. Active listening and probing questions may reveal that the prescribed antibiotic is costly and that Mr. Keyes believes he is demonstrating thrift and foresight by saving half of the prescription. As a partner in his pet's care, you can help him to administer the best possible treatment.

Notes

1. J. Shirley. The Art of Listening: A Forgotten Tool. *AAHA Trends*, Mar 1992: 39–40.
2. D. Goleman. All Too Often, the Doctor Isn't Listening, Studies Show. *New York Times*, Nov 13, 1992: 1.
3. S. Brown et al. *Patient Satisfaction Pays: Quality Service for Practice Success.* Gaithersburg, MD: Aspen Publications, 1993.

Action Steps for Building Rapport and Creating a Partnership

1. Read the client's chart before entering the exam room, and make a note of something personal on which to comment.

2. Give each client your undivided, caring attention during the exam or consultation.

3. Ask clients what they want or expect from the visit, and at the conclusion ask if their needs have been met.

4. Ask open-ended questions; they are interactive and elicit information that "yes–no" questions can't. Don't interrupt.

5. Show interest by establishing eye contact, and don't write in the chart every moment you're with the client.

6. Encourage informed client partners by giving them information for decision making.

7. Try to give clients options and consequences and to gain their agreement regarding the pet's treatment plan.

8. Emphasize to your clients that the doctor-client relationship is a partnership in which the client has an equal responsibility with the veterinarian to gain the best outcome for the pet.

4.   K. Bertakis et al. *The Relationship*: 175–181. The Relationship of Physician Medical Interview Style to Patient Satisfaction, *Journal of Family Practice* 32(2), 1991:175–181.
5.   D. Scott. *Client Satisfaction: The Other Half of Your Job*. Menlo Park, CA: Crisp Publications/AVMA 1998: 81–90.
6.   E. J. Emanuel and L. L. Emanuel. "Four Models of the Veterinarian-Client Relationship, *Journal of the Medical Association*, 267(16) 1992: 2221–2226.

Chapter 14

Client Retention Strategies

The client is not always right, but the client is always the client.[1]

You've gotten your client past the phone and the schedule, communicated clearly, and established a working partnership. If you thought you were finished, though, think again. Follow-up and follow-through are essential to keep clients coming back.

Plenty of details occur after the office visit that will compel your clients to send you their friends, coworkers, and neighbors or that will propel them to another practice. These after-the-exam details may seem like minor matters, but they can have a major impact on client retention.

Routine follow-up is one thing, but what do you do about client complaints? Your clients don't complain, you say? They may not complain to *you*, but they certainly do tell their friends and neighbors. Your ability to ferret out and resolve complaints—as well as prevent them—has a major impact on client referrals and client retention. Let's take a look at some ideas for enhancing customer satisfaction after your clients leave the exam room.

Being a Well-Pet Advocate

How is your vaccination reminder system working? With increasing media coverage of vaccination problems, and the perceived competition from low-cost vaccine clinics, smart veterinarians emphasize the annual physical examination to remind clients of the value they receive from their visit.

Clients like this Tennessee cat and dog owner agree that annual physical exams are necessary.

> *Oh, yes, they're important. I wouldn't want anything to happen to my pets. They need their shots. The vet cleans the ears, checks for worms, and checks for mites at the same time.*

Tailor your reminders to each patient: the geriatric dog or cat, puppy and kitten reminders, and notes of concern for specific breeds.

Says Dr. Robert Cartin:

> *Instead of sending out reminder postcards, we send out letters. I like that because we can add extra information, such as an explanation about a new vaccine. We may spend a couple more cents on postage, but people are going to open it up.*

Others may find that a postcard works best. Tailor your approach to your clients. Dr. Ross Clark recommends using your computer to sort and select for certain factors, sending a letter to one group a month explaining the origin, expected behavior, and potential medical problems of that particular breed or type of pet.[2] You might send breeders a special newsletter, or send messages to selected clients recommending dental exams and prophylaxis for their pets.

Once the client brings in the pet for its exam, explain why a dog of this breed or a cat of this age needs special attention, laboratory tests, or more frequent exams. Emphasize that spotting problems before they become severe reduces the animal's discomfort and saves money.

For instance, a Washington veterinarian makes a point of educating owners of Cocker Spaniel puppies about ear care: "Educating and preparing clients reduces their frustration during the following years, when dogs of that breed tend to develop more ear problems than other dogs."

Adding Warmth to Follow-up Care

Make appointments for clients to pick up animals that have been hospitalized or had surgery, rather than having them just "drop in" to take their pets home. Clients are reassured when a veterinarian or technician personally reviews with them the surgery and take-home instructions. And you can be sure that the client doesn't slip away without receiving vital information.

Placing a call 48 to 72 hours after every visit is useful in determining the pet's response to any treatment or the owner's difficulty in administering medications. Likewise, call clients after their pet's surgery or hospitalization, after you've prescribed a new medication with potential side effects, and after consultation with referral veterinarians. Some veterinarians send get-well cards for pets that are sent home after hospitalization.

Record on the veterinary chart every client contact, whether it is in person, by letter, by telephone, by you or by a staff member. Your call shows concern and continuity of care between providers, and it may head off problems before they develop. After a client's first visit, designate a technician or assistant—or, ideally, the veterinarian—to call the client at home. This informal, friendly call might go something like this:

> *Mr. Smith? This is Dr. Goodhealth. I was just calling to see if any questions or concerns came to you after you left our practice today. And I wanted to know if you think there is anything we could have done better or differently during your visit.*

When a client calls with a problem over the weekend and speaks with your associate or a relief veterinarian, call the client yourself the following Monday. This shows that you and your associates work as a team and that you're concerned about your clients.

At Owl Creek Veterinary Hospital in Virginia Beach, VA, implementing a callback policy actually saved staff time by cutting down the number of daily calls made to the reception desk. At first, clients were called only after their pets had a surgical procedure, but now every client is called after every visit.[3]

Quieting Lab Result Jitters

How do you report lab results? Are clients expected to call you? Do you call them? Waiting for lab results can be agonizing for clients. Does the cat have diabetes or kidney failure? Is the lump malignant? Think about how you would react to such unnerving concerns if you were the client. Then think about how you would deal with worrying over a long holiday weekend while your doctor is out of town or while the lab results make their way across town by wagon train to the clinic.

Do you offer in-house laboratory testing for quick results? If not, tell your clients what to expect in the way of getting results. If the time frame usually is 3 days, tell them it will be 5 days. Periodically compare lab turn-around times and accuracy of results. If the lab you use is not providing fast, accurate service, find another one. The lab you use reflects the quality of your service.

If you're still using the "no news is good news" system of informing clients, reconsider it. More than one lawsuit in human medicine has been won by a patient who was told, "We'll call you if there's a problem on your lab test," when in fact the lack of a telephone call meant that the lab work was lost or the report was misplaced. Keeping a lab log that includes a check-off for having delivered the result assures client notification and provides a fail-safe mechanism for detecting lost samples.

Staying in Touch Between Visits

Many practices send newsletters to clients as a way to keep in touch, to send along information about keeping their pets healthy, to comment on the latest veterinary news, and to personalize the practice with news of staff and veterinarians. Is this communication technique worth the time and expense? Ask anyone who has discontinued a practice newsletter whether it's effective. If it was a regularly mailed and well-done publication, people miss it when it's gone. Clients appreciate this subtle reminder of the practice even if they never comment on it.

What do you do about clients who use low-cost vaccine clinics for routine care but come to you for other medical and surgical care? According to the *AAHA Report*, most pet owners believe it's important to keep all their pets' records in one place.[4] Emphasize this, and ask them for vaccination dates even if the procedure is done elsewhere. You then can enter the information into your reminder system for the next year.

Dr. Cartin finds that working with low-cost clinics actually helps his business:

> *Several places nearby do vaccines and very basic care, and we have a good relationship with them. We have them give their clients a certificate for a free exam with us. Granted, I've lost some vaccine income, but we're getting clients. These discount places see a lot of people with pet problems, and they're the gatekeepers who can send the clients on to our practice. Some of the doctors here think we're doing free work, but [in my view] it's a form of advertising and marketing.*

"Thank You's" to Keep Referrals Coming

Thank anyone who refers clients to you. All referrals, whether they come from clients, friends, or other veterinarians, merit a friendly note saying, "Thank you for recommending me. I appreciate your trust."

"We encourage client referrals by giving a fifteen-dollar credit for referring someone," says Dr. Thomas Austin. "We want them to know we appreciate referrals. That's a major source of business for us."

Keep your referring veterinarians informed of their clients' progress, too, and not only with the standard "Thank you for referring Ms. Jones" letter that describes the diagnosis and treatment. If treatment is protracted or involved, send copies of lab and diagnostic test results and interim progress reports, and let your client know that you are keeping the referring veterinarian informed in this way. This communication not only keeps referrals coming but also lets the client know of the continuity of care between primary and referral veterinarians.

Extending Condolences

When a pet dies, what do you do? Some veterinarians send a sympathy card or flowers. Others make a memorial contribution in the name of a deceased pet. A staff member at one clinic makes a clay paw print from the deceased pet and sends it to the owners along with a card. [5]

The decision for euthanasia is a difficult one. Dr. Nancy Murbach, owner of Housecall Veterinary Service in Scottsdale, AZ, has developed a plan for these situations.

> *If I don't know the pet and its history well, I do a thorough physical exam and take a history so that I'm comfortable with the decision to euthanize. Sometimes people come to the decision unaware that the pet has a treatable condition and are very grateful when alternatives are offered. Often, people do not acknowledge that they have a choice at this time. I believe we owe it to them and their pets to make sure they understand and are provided the options. One older male dog had a significant prostatitis. With treatment, he responded quickly and completely and lived two more years.*
>
> *As a housecall veterinarian I've found the ideal setting for the majority of euthanasias. My goals are to avoid upsetting the pet and to make it as pleasant as possible for the owner. I spend a lot of time talking to the owners. We may talk about how long they have had the pet, some of the things it used to do, and other memories. I give children the choice of being present or not. Most choose to remain and are a source of strength for their parents. If the pet is alert, I give a sedative first. I administer the euthanasia solution through the lateral saphenous vein so the owners can hug and talk to the pet at the same time.*
>
> *It's best to discuss disposal before the euthanasia. I may offer to assist with a home burial, cremation, or transport of the animal's remains. Having a plan for the entire process seems to help people get through it. Afterward, I send a condolence card that includes*

some thoughts about the pet. I make a follow-up phone call to owners who have had a hard time dealing with the loss of the pet or their decision to euthanize. I also make a donation to my veterinary college in the pet's memory. Pet owners tell me they appreciate this gesture.

The option of euthanasia is both a blessing and a heartache for veterinarians and clients alike. Although the process is never easy, having a plan eases the difficulty for everyone.

Retaining Clients

Follow-up after routine visits is one thing, but what do you do about disgruntled clients? In the next chapter we'll address the issue of service recovery, the art of making wrongs right. Often, though, a client complaint is a result of a misunderstanding about billing.

Fees are a sore point with veterinarians and clients alike. The reality is that fees will always be a problem for some people. Although some pet owners gripe about fees, the importance of their complaint is often overrated.

They're expensive, but everybody is. I won't change; I'm happy. —Massachusetts pet owner

In a life-threatening situation, I'd take my pet to a vet in town who charges more [than my regular vet]; she's better. —California client

I couldn't believe that my vet only charged me $7 to express my dog's anal sacs. Of all things that people don't want to do themselves! And then he said he'd only charge me $5 for the next time, since my dog needs to have it done so often. I was shocked. He does that with other clients, too. What he doesn't realize is that they'd all pay more, because they love him. —Oregon multiple-pet owner

According to an AAHA study, more than half of pet owners could not remember how much they paid for their pets' vaccinations. Of the 50% of pet owners who have ever switched veterinarians, only 7% said they did

Client Concerns About Fees

To reduce client concerns:

✦ Provide written estimates for all procedures and for all clients.

✦ Explain the reasons for your fees, to give clients a sense of value for their money spent. If you're charging $22 to set up an IV and to continuously monitor an animal's response to administration of fluids, don't say you're charging $22 "for fluids."

✦ Let clients know that any financial concerns can be discussed freely and privately with your practice manager. Post a sign to that effect in the reception area, and place business cards nearby. Tell clients that if they have a problem with a bill, they can call your practice manager.

✦ Although many veterinarians post signs in their reception areas saying, "Payment is expected at time of service unless other arrangements are made," others still are willing to bill clients. If you do so, have clients fill out a credit application form that defines your agreement.

so to get lower prices.[6] Nonetheless, your clients want to know how their money is being spent.

> When my dog was in renal failure and had to have fluids every day, my vet charged me $22 a bag. I knew the real cost was nowhere near that. Inquiries at the pharmacy revealed that I could order a case of 10 for $46. I felt, and still feel, resentful of such a horrendous price markup. —Ohio client

Veterinarians focusing on prices may be missing the source of their clients' main concerns. The relationship between veterinarians, pets, and pet owners is of primary importance to veterinary clients. Review the previous chapter to be sure you've established a solid partnership with your clients. When creating payment policies, do what makes sense for you and your clients as long as it keeps your accounts receivable at a reasonable level. (Accounts receivable, properly managed and accompanied by interest or billing fees, can add rather than subtract revenue.)

As said by Marilyn Bergquist, CAE:

*Research shows that price is not the number one
reason for resistance. It may be the number-one
reason expressed, however, because it's very easy to
say, "Gee, that seems so expensive." What does the
client have to lose by saying that? Absolutely
nothing, and everything to gain: You may lower the
price!*

*Discussions on pricing make everyone
uncomfortable. If the price is given as a reason,
what that means is that you have not explained the
value of the recommendation to the client.[7]*

Attending to Small Concerns

Many other issues can sweeten or sour a client's
relationship with you. Inefficient office procedures,
incomplete follow-up, and unresolved problems can all
lead a client to less-than-positive conclusions about your
practice, even when you've done a good job of communicating and partnering with your clients and their pets.

Dr. Paul Glouton keeps small problems from escalating
by calling clients after they've been to his hospital, and
again when their pet's treatment should be complete.

*Sometimes you'll find the treatment didn't really
work the way they thought it would, and they're
looking to call someone else. If you call back, it
gives you the chance to clear up the problem.[8]*

The book *In Search of Excellence* points out that top
managers treat service problems as "real-time" issues
that deserve immediate, personal attention.[9] There's
something to be said for that philosophy, and satisfied
clients will say it. In the next chapter we'll show you
how to respond quickly and appropriately when mistakes
happen.

Notes

1. D. Scott. *Client Satisfaction: The Other Half of Your Job.* Menlo Park, CA: Crisp Publications/AVMA, 1998: 59, 71–73.
2. R. Clark. *Mastering the Marketplace: Taking Your Practice to the Top.* Lenexa, KS: Veterinary Medicine Publishing Group, 1996: 19.
3. A. Ashby. Grow Your Practice. *AAHA Trends*, May 1995: 17–19.

Action Steps for Client Retention

1. Know what happens when clients leave the exam room. Follow-up is important to your clients' perception of care.

2. Give clients hands-on education in administering medication, changing bandages, and other at-home treatments.

3. Call clients at home after their pet's surgery or acute illness.

4. Be a well-pet advocate.

5. Stay in touch between visits with phone calls or a newsletter.

6. Thank those who send you referral clients, and when you send a client to a referral veterinarian, find out his or her perception of the veterinarian.

7. Send a get-well or sympathy card when a pet is hospitalized or dies.

8. Provide a knowledgeable person and a private place for clients to discuss financial matters.

4. American Animal Hospital Association. *1995 AAHA Report: A Study of the Companion Animal Veterinary Services Market*: 109–111.
5. Pearls of Practice: Business Ideas and Insights for the Veterinary Hospital Team. *Veterinary Economics FirstLine*, Oct/Nov 1997: 7.
6. *1995 AAHA Report*.
7. M. Bergquist. The Reluctant Client. *AAHA Trends*, Sep 1993: 27.
8. K. L. Czepiel. They're Calling Us — Why Aren't They Asking You? *AAHA Trends*, Jan 1997: 21–22.
9. T. J. Peters and R. H. Waterman, Jr. *In Search of Excellence: Lessons from America's Best-Run Companies*. New York: Harper and Row, 1982: 166.

Chapter 15

Service Recovery for Loyal Clients

An error gracefully acknowledged is a victory won.—Caroline L. Gascoigne

When you make a mistake so horrible that it is to die over, don't.—Oscar London, MD[1]

No matter how well organized a practice, how understanding and knowledgeable the staff, or how quality oriented the attitude, mistakes will happen. Make no mistake about it. Whether it's a result of a mix-up, memory gap, miscommunication, or misunderstanding, someone will misplace a chart, record an appointment at the wrong time, forget to make a phone call, overcharge, or keep someone waiting too long. In a practice that is moving toward empowerment and innovation, mistakes may occur even more frequently at first as employees become accustomed to making decisions independently.

Sometimes a complaint is the result of miscommunication, lack of clarification, or overuse of jargon on the part of veterinarian or staff. A complaint may be directed at you even though the problem lies with clinical problems that are beyond anyone's control, such as slow recovery or side effects of medication. No matter why the complaint comes about, who is at fault, or how minor the problem, it requires attention.

Figure 15.1 The Triple-A Action Plan

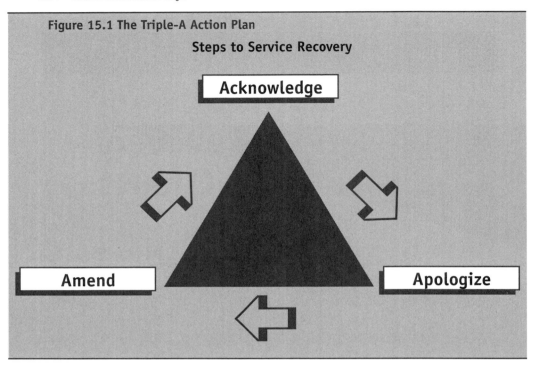

Steps to Service Recovery

Acknowledge

Amend

Apologize

The error is not necessarily in the mistake itself but, instead, in not acknowledging it, making amends, and trying to prevent future mistakes. Clients tell us (and consumer research confirms) that service errors are forgivable if they are not predictable (that is, if the same or similar mistakes don't happen routinely) and if the organization or individual who made the mistake acknowledges it, apologizes for it, and makes amends. The process of acknowledging and correcting errors is called *service recovery*.

The Triple-A Action Plan

Service recovery doesn't deny the error, but it allows the practice to learn from it while reinstating client satisfaction. A recovery strategy, even one as simple as an apology, actually can turn clients into strong advocates for the practice.

Recovery does not mean that clients should be told about every clinical error. Revealing veterinary misdiagnosis, incorrect procedures, inaccurate test interpretation, or other clinical mistakes should be approached judiciously and sometimes only after consulting your attorney or insurer. If you have developed a good rapport with your client, if you make a habit of communicating thoroughly and personally, and if the error is not the result of sloppiness, laziness, or attempting something you are not fully trained to do, your chances of incurring a malpractice liability suit are minimized. We call the steps in service recovery the Triple-A Action Plan (see Figure 15.1).

Acknowledge the Mistake

When a mistake or misunderstanding happens, no matter who is at fault, the first step is to acknowledge the error and the wronged party's right to be concerned or angry. Acknowledging the problem (without necessarily accepting blame, unless you are clearly at fault) defuses the situation without diminishing the individual's right to be upset.

In acknowledging the situation, thank the client for bringing an unsatisfactory, disruptive, or disappointing situation to your attention. Turn problems over to the practice team, as appropriate, or to an ad hoc team, to analyze and solve. Even sticky or embarrassing problems should be addressed.

In *Beyond Customer Service*,[2] Richard Gerson notes that service recovery requires you to:

- ✦ Understand
- ✦ Listen
- ✦ Handle one complaint at a time, even if the client has several
- ✦ Empathize

Apologize

Saying "I'm sorry" is a critical step in service recovery. For example: "Mr. Garcia, I'm very sorry I didn't call you with the lab results promptly as I promised. I had to treat an emergency and was unable to call you, but I should have made arrangements for someone else to contact you. I know you're angry, and I apologize for inconveniencing you."

As in acknowledgment, apologizing does not require that you accept blame unless the practice is at fault for the problem. It may consist of a simple, "I'm sorry this situation occurred" or, "I'm sorry you had to wait." An apology conveys concern, which is one of the key characteristics that clients seek from veterinarians and staff members. If there's even the slightest question as to whether something went wrong, apologize anyway. You can't go wrong, and your client will be impressed.

Amend

To handle an irate person, solve the problem without blaming yourself or others.—Dru Scott[3]

No matter how seemingly minor the error may be, a demonstration of contrition conveys grace and sincerity. Making amends can be simple but heartfelt, such as a hand-written note of apology. If the error is more severe (a client arrived for her dog's ultrasound appointment only to discover that it hadn't been recorded in the schedule, yet she has a card that was given to her when she made the appointment), making amends may require working the client into the schedule, discounting the bill, sending a green plant to her home or office, or a similar display of apology.

To captivate the client, do something unexpected or beyond what's called for. Think of the impact when the client tells 15 curious coworkers, "The flowers are from my veterinarian. His office had promised to call in the morning with some important test results, and they didn't call until the next day."

Dru Scott recommends first asking the client what he or she wants, then outlining the solution or alternatives.[4] Making amends often means presenting options to the offended party. A common action in veterinary practice is to offer to a client whose appointment time has been delayed the option of waiting or rescheduling for another day. People like being given choices because it gives them a feeling of control. Conversely, when people feel they have no control over a situation, they are more likely to get angry when an error is made. You can maintain your own sense of control by defining the choices that you offer.

Two basic requirements accompany the Amend step of the Triple-A Action Plan for service recovery:

1. Employees must convey sincere concern and interest upon learning of a problem.

2. They must be empowered to solve problems and make amends.

Nothing is more irritating to a client than to be told, "I'm so sorry, Mr. Wiu, but I'm not authorized to change a billing statement. I'll have to talk to the practice manager, and she'll have to check with Dr. Zimmerman. We'll call you next week."

Instead of saying "I can't do that," tell the client what you *will* do. Even if you can't solve the problem immediately, you still can still say, "I'll look up the records and call you back in 5 minutes" or "I'll go talk to the receptionist immediately if you'll have a seat in the conference room."

Christine Cooley, phone operator for Newport Harbor Animal Hospital, says:

> *A lot of times we do go out of our way for the client and do whatever it takes. The other day a client had prepaid for something and had a friend come down and pick up the prescription. When the friend came down, the receptionist didn't realize that the client had already prepaid, so the friend wrote a check, and then when the friend told the client, she called and was upset. I ended up driving the check over to her home to make her happy because she was so upset, and by the time I got there, she was almost embarrassed that she was so upset. But she was so happy that I had offered to drive it over. That probably saved her as a client.*

The Triple-A Action Plan for service recovery is meaningful and effective if it's required only occasionally to deal with one-of-a-kind errors. If you or someone in the practice deals consistently with the same problems (same situation, different faces), this may be a sign of a bigger problem—unclear communication, processes without ownership, or unempowered employees, for instance. When a service error occurs more than once, it's wise to look behind the symptom to find the source of the error.

When a mistake occurs, the *person*(s) who made it should not be criticized. This may inhibit future decision making and innovation. Instead, critique the *process* that caused the problem, and institute a process for recovery and prevention.

Encouraging Clients and Staff To Speak Up

Although some clients are happy to mention their displeasure to anyone they encounter, others may withhold this information, fearing that the receptionist will get in trouble or the doctor's feelings will be hurt. Smart veterinarians view complaining customers as an asset because they provide the opportunity to improve. Let clients know you want to hear their complaints. A threat-free environment must exist for clients or staff to feel comfortable in pointing out a problem or a mistake.

A study of customer complaining behavior showed that customers often don't complain because they believe the process is complex and time-consuming and that the result is not worth it. Sometimes they don't complain because they believe nothing will result from it. These customers leave, taking their referral potential with them.[5]

To encourage clients to disclose problems and provide suggestions, make it easy for them, and make it clear that effective action will follow (see Chapter 3 for ideas). Some practices use a complaint form to collect information about the problem—how it was resolved, by whom, and with what results—along with recommendations for changes in procedures. In larger practices a formal system for tracking and following up on client complaints may be implemented (the form should not be used as an excuse for delaying immediate action, though).

Instruct your staff members to bring problems to your attention, and don't deny the problem, belittle its importance, point fingers, or punish them when they do. Some veterinary hospitals monitor client satisfaction with an "incident reporting system" that encourages reports from any staff member on anything that goes amiss, from a lack of toilet paper in the bathroom to a dog that lunges at a cat in the waiting room. Follow-up action is required for each report. Encourage everyone within the practice to participate in ferreting out errors, determining the root cause, and responding immediately to service errors.

Client Exit Interviews

Dr. Robert Cartin reported that:

> We had a request for a records transfer from a client whose dog had skin problems. These clients took their daughter to a physician, who diagnosed scabies and told them the dog must have given it to her. They assumed we had missed the diagnosis. I got the record and called them and told them I'd be happy to scrape the skin and treat it at no charge. They came in and were happy with the follow-up.

How do *you* follow up when a client leaves the practice? If a request for transfer of records to another local veterinarian comes in, do you simply transfer the records without question? In smart practices either the veterinarian or the practice manager contacts the client, conducting telephone exit interviews or sending a personal letter with a survey to determine the source of dissatisfaction.

Express regret that the client wishes to leave the practice, and show interest in learning how the practice might improve and prevent further errors. Begin with, "We received and will honor your request to transfer your records. We're sorry you're leaving our practice and hope you will share with us your reasons for the change."

If you tell clients immediately that you will honor their request, they will feel less pressured. Let them know that you'll keep the permanent record and will make copies for whomever the client requests. You then can find out the reasons for their request, offer solutions, and give them the choice of returning to your practice.

The client should be told that his or her honest and candid responses will be used to correct problems in action or attitude. If the client is hesitant to respond, and if questioning does not elicit clarification, encourage the client to put the complaint in writing. Send a form and a stamped self-addressed envelope to make it easy to do so.

This can be an enlightening experience. You may learn things you don't know about your staff, your style, your fee structure, and other matters. A call to a departing client may reveal that your receptionist treated her rudely or that the client was offended by the way you brushed off her questions about herbal treatments.

When You Can't Do Enough

Occasionally you may encounter a client who just can't be pleased. The best "service" you may offer them is to direct them elsewhere. Dr. Cartin says:

> We probably do about three letters a year that we call "dump" letters, where we say that although we try to please every client, we apparently are not meeting their goals, so we ask them to seek services elsewhere.

Mark Opperman suggests that you "discharge" these clients. Take them into a room and explain that you are unable to meet their needs and, therefore, you recommend that they obtain services from another veterinary hospital. Removing these people from your client base, he says, may do wonders for everyone's morale.[6]

Before you place a client is in this category, make an extra effort to ensure that you've done all you can to listen, understand, and empathize with him or her. If you have several of these kinds of clients, the problem may be you, not them.

Planning for Recovery

To realize that a problem exists and target a plan for improvement is not enough. The plan must be monitored to be certain that change occurs and sticks. Slipping back into bad habits and traditional ways of handling a process is easy to do. Be sure to incorporate routine "checkups" into action plans and service recovery processes.

Action Steps for Service Recovery

1. Accept that mistakes will occur, and institute a service recovery strategy.

2. Create a threat-free environment to encourage everyone—clients, staff, vendors, and referral source—to point out service errors.

3. Empower employees to take appropriate action immediately.

4. Identify the source of the mistake to prevent recurrences. Provide methods by which to bring out errors: surveys, suggestion boxes, personal follow-up, exit interviews.

5. Criticize and correct the *process*, not the person.

6. When a records transfer is requested, do an exit interview to find out why the client is leaving.

Dr. Cartin notes:

Our receptionist refers to difficult clients as "an opportunity." If you can swing those people over and they come back, that's a good sign.

Striving for service excellence demands effective and caring follow-up, including a service recovery process. Effective follow-through keeps clients coming back. A service recovery strategy says, "We care about what our customers think. We aren't perfect, but we'll work continually and consistently to get there."

Notes

1. O. London. *Kill As Few Patients As Possible and 56 Other Essays on How To Be the World's Best Doctor.* Berkeley, CA.: Ten-Speed Press, 1987: 5–6.
2. R. Gerson. *Beyond Customer Service: Keeping Clients for Life.* Menlo Park, CA: Crisp Publications/AVMA, 1993/1994: 45–46.
3. D. Scott. *Client Satisfaction: The Other Half of Your Job.* Menlo Park, CA: Crisp Publications/AVMA, 1998: 59, 71–73.
4. Scott.
5. J. A. Goodman, T. Marra, and L. Brigham. Customer Service: Costly Nuisance or Low-cost Profit Strategy? *Journal of Retail Banking,* Fall 1986: 716
6. M. Opperman. Don't Let Explosive Clients Disrupt Your Practice! *Veterinary Economics,* Sept 1995: 76–79.

Chapter 16

Quality Is A Moving Target

Call them what you want—customers...
passengers...patients...clients...These are the
people who buy and use the products you sell or
the services you provide. Sometimes they make
work a pleasure, and sometimes they're hard as
nails. Day in, day out, they make you earn your
money.—Price Pritchett[1]

It's time to wrap up what you've learned, summarize what we've covered, and get to work. Client satisfaction isn't a step-by-step process with a beginning and an end. It's a moving target that requires continual effort by you and your practice team. You'll find that you return to these pages as time goes on and as you raise your standards for client satisfaction.

Why You're Here

Once again we want to emphasize a point that we and other veterinarians have made throughout this book: Quality service and client satisfaction are worth the effort. You'll see the payoff in the practice bottom line and professional satisfaction. These factors begin and end with your belief and your commitment. A continuing, visible commitment is the only way to achieve service that consistently satisfies and frequently surpasses expectations. What we're saying is that you must know what you believe. Does this sound simple? Perhaps, but in far too many practices the employees (and sometimes the veterinarians) can give no specific, consensus response to the question, "Why are you here?"

If a practice team is to provide quality service, strive to exceed expectations, and give quality veterinary care, the team members must agree and sincerely believe that the client comes first. Everyone in the practice—the bookkeeper, veterinary assistant, technician, part-time janitor, receptionist, and of course the veterinarians—must share this belief.

Think of this as the beginning rather than the end. Meeting the needs of your clients, as you know now, is a day-to-day, moment-to-moment process. Even though you provide quality care with your veterinary expertise and technique, it's predicated on attentive, personal interaction with the entire staff. Ensuring satisfied clients is the role and responsibility of everyone in the practice, and the rewards of practice success belong to everyone who participates: clients, staff, and veterinarians.

No Cookie Cutter for Quality

There's no one perfect way to practice medicine. Still, you should strive for the best quality of veterinary care and service. We have encountered plenty of veterinarians and practices with a unique style in everything from scheduling and billing to interactions with clients. What works for you and exceeds client expectations is the best way, as this story illustrates:

When I was still in high school, we lived on a small farm and always had lots of cats. If one of our barn cats became ill, too bad. My dad said if anything was going to spend the night in a hospital, it was going to be a cow or a pig (our meat supply!). One day, I found one of the cats very ill in the barn. He was so sick that his eyes were rolling around in his head and he was coughing and had a snotty nose. Of course, Dad said he'd just have to die—no vet!

Still being in school, I didn't have my own money, but I called up a vet (actually, it was the first woman vet anyone in our area had heard of) and, sobbing uncontrollably, told her my life story and that I had no money. She told me if I could get my cat to the office, she would give me antibiotics and show me how to administer them. My mom agreed to take me there on the way to school, and the kindly vet, Dr. Samuelson, gave me the antibiotics and told me to call her with updates of my ill cat. I'll never forget that. Checkers recovered fully, thanks to her.

Do you get the impression that you don't create client satisfaction and quality service by using a cookie cutter? You're right. Every practice and every veterinarian has a unique style, and you can maintain that style if you've first determined that it doesn't undermine your ability to provide excellent veterinary care and superior service and to exceed client expectations.

Continuous Improvement

Continuous improvement as a formal business growth strategy is a relatively new concept in the United States. Significantly, the English language does not have a single word to express the concept of continuous improvement, whereas the Japanese understand its value and processes culturally and linguistically, using the word *kaizan* to express it. Although we don't have a succinct way to say it, client-centered practices understand the importance of continuous improvement. The veterinarians and staff in these practices talk and share ideas among themselves, formally and informally. They look for other practices and other firms against which to benchmark, and they look for problems before clients call their attention to them.

These practices, and the veterinarians who lead them, take an emphatic stance where client satisfaction is concerned. They believe, and act on the belief, that clients are paramount in the practice. They ensure a client orientation by hiring, training, continually educating, and constantly motivating and rewarding staff members. In these practices, improving client satisfaction and finding ways to bring it to an even higher level are topics of frequent discussion and action.

Quality doesn't stand still. It's why you attend veterinary meetings and conferences regularly. Medicine is changing, improving, continually finding new therapies and procedures that will keep pets healthy. Techniques that seemed perfectly reasonable 10 years ago—or even yesterday—may seem prehistoric tomorrow. Service quality is just the same. It demands continually "upping the bar," looking for ways to satisfy client needs a little more thoroughly, a little more personally, a little more efficiently.

Continuous improvement calls for setting standards, monitoring what's working (and what's not), fixing things that go wrong and preventing them from happening again, paying attention to clients, looking at other practices, other businesses, other industries. Continuity is the continuing education of service— continuous improvement for practice success.

A "Good Enough Isn't" Attitude

An innovative, client-oriented team—the team you and your staff now are, or are on your way to becoming— must constantly look for ways to provide better service and soar above client expectations. This service attitude is akin to cardiovascular conditioning. Newly quality-conscious organizations are like novice runners. At first, the daily run of 1 or 2 miles leaves them gasping and fatigued, but eventually they build endurance so that 3 or 5 miles becomes routine. Then they begin looking for challenges—hills, a faster pace, more miles to cover, a 10K race, even a marathon in which to test themselves. Seasoned runners continually seek improvement. When they break 3 hours in a marathon, they strive for 2:50. They become conditioned to achieve.

If you're intent on achieving client satisfaction, no one—veterinarians or staff—can be satisfied with the most recent accomplishment or accolade. Enjoy it, then move on, striving for service excellence through im-proved processes.

Like runners seeking constantly to improve their cardiovascular condition, pace, and running style, you and your staff must build on each success in the practice. Look for small steps you can take toward better care and better service. This should be a regular topic of discussion at staff meetings and during departmental, committee, and veterinarian meetings. Make it a specific responsibility of every member of the practice; write it into job descriptions to reinforce the expectation that quality is everyone's job.

Don't leave "well enough" alone. Improve it. Then work on making it better still. Set standards for waiting time, client education, communication, billing, return calls, and all other areas of your practice. Monitor client and staff expectations and reactions. When you find that you're consistently reaching the standards you've set, move the bar a little higher.

Like the ultra-fit athlete who runs compulsively every day, rain or shine, this continual striving for improvement has measurable benefits. It doesn't matter if you are the best doctor with the best diagnosis; if the client is dissatisfied because of the way the receptionist talked to her, or if your rapport with the client is poor, or the client is not handled politely on the phone, the client will go back and report to her family, "I don't care for that veterinarian." That could be the end of that relationship.

Small Is Big

Says an Ohio pet owner:

> My dog was very sick with heart disease and other problems just before Memorial Day weekend. My vet was very concerned as we headed into the holiday, so for that weekend, he called twice a day to see how Dusty was doing. That type of attention in a pending crisis was really appreciated.

Practices that take service seriously regard minor matters as major concerns. They are fanatic about client service, as are the veterinarians and staff at Clocktower Animal Hospital when they clean off the fingerprints on their hospital windows each morning.

Is this "small is big" attitude excessive? It may be fanatic, but it's not excessive. "Service fanatics" are people who say, "Good enough isn't," who believe that tiny complaints, ignored because they're believed to be insignificant, pile up to create an immovable mountain. They believe it's better to pick up a few rocks in the road than to let them accumulate to the point that you need a backhoe.

People in these practices look for barriers early on, querying clients, referral sources, staff members, and each other. They analyze and evaluate every aspect of their practice and their service, from accessibility of the bathrooms to clarity of their instructions. They offer countless opportunities for clients and staff to speak up and speak out by using suggestion boxes, follow-up phone calls, question cards, and visit-concluding "anything else?" questions. They don't stop there. They fix the glitches and goof-ups by using the knowledge they gain from the repair process; they regard mistakes as a classroom for learning and improvement.

The veterinarians, practice managers, and staff members with whom we spoke take a fervent approach to service. Like a house cleaned by an army of white-glove house-keepers, these practices sparkle physically and emotionally. The veterinarians and staff seem happier than the typical practice, and their clients radiate enthusiastic satisfaction.

The purpose of this continuous attention is prevention. Look for problems to prevent, and you'll find opportunities to improve. When clients are regarded as customers in a practice, and when customers are moved to the top of the organization chart, veterinarians and staff take on a whole new attitude. It's an attitude we noticed in our interviews and visits. In practices and organizations such as these, there's an aura that says, "You're special," not "We're special." The focus is on the customer.

The Real Rewards of Communication and Education

Quality-oriented practices understand the value of communication. They communicate up, down, and across all lines and segments of the practice. They hold regular staff meetings, team meetings, and unit meetings. Veterinarians and staff meet together and separately. They talk formally and informally. They emphasize quality by reviewing and praising incidents that were handled well and by discussing those that were not. Then they figure out what they should do or change. They compliment each other when things go right and help each other when times are tough.

These practices not only communicate but also have fun and celebrate together. High-quality practices are places where stress sometimes reaches outrageous levels. These practices destress with laughter. They understand that humor distracts and provides a new perspective. Tom Peters, coauthor of *In Search of Excellence*, counsels (and we concur) that the "top dogs" must participate with the rest of the team.[2]

At Town and Country Veterinary Clinic in Gulfport, MS, the hospital supplies lunch once a month for staff members when they meet to work on problem solving or to be educated on new topics.[3] Practices such as these, in which client satisfaction is a targeted objective, spend an incredible amount of time communicating with each other. Seldom did we encounter a practice whose practice manager or veterinarians said, "We don't have time for staff meetings." These practices meet in groups of two or 10 or 30 and more—daily, weekly, monthly, or annually, depending on the purpose of the meeting and the members of the group. They meet to communicate, to share ideas, and to take action.

Practices that are client-centered understand that an educated, informed staff gives better care and better service. The practices we visited make a significant commitment to staff development, offering monthly educational programs on clinical as well as personal growth topics.

Trends

We originally planned to tell you, "This won't hurt a bit," but we changed our plan. The future of veterinary medicine is too unpredictable for us to say it won't hurt. No matter what happens to veterinary care in the next decade, it's likely to be somewhat painful for everyone. It will be painful in the sense that change is always painful. And, although no one can predict with certainty what the future will bring, it's fairly safe to assume that the transformations witnessed in the past decade are only the beginning of change.

Despite these uncertainties, we feel confident about this prediction: Satisfying clients will be the hallmark of successful veterinary practices and professionally fulfilled veterinarians through the next century. Successful veterinarians listen to their clients. They talk to their colleagues. They pay attention to what's going on in the world around them. They anticipate trends rather than try to catch up with them.

What trends should you be anticipating? What trends will influence your practice in the coming years? What realities may be affecting your practice already? Here's what you might expect:

✦ Changing demographics and psychographics of society with the aging of the Baby Boomer generation, the burgeoning number of elderly people, and increased multicultural diversity

✦ Decreasing emphasis on and income from vaccinations

✦ Increasing emphasis on physical exams and geriatric animal care

✦ Increasing numbers of large or "corporate" practices

✦ Increasing interest in pet health insurance and pet wellness/health-care plans

✦ Increasing use of computers and online technology for both business and medical (e.g., "telemedicine") purposes

Each of these trends will affect how veterinary services are developed, delivered, and assessed. They will influence how you practice medicine and how clients pay for their services. How you respond to these changes will determine not only how successful you will be financially but also how satisfied you will be in your chosen profession.

We sincerely believe that, by centering your practice on your clients, you will renew the satisfaction and fulfillment that compelled you to choose veterinary medicine as a profession. By viewing your clients as customers and caring about them as people, you center your own life professionally and personally.

Customizing Client Satisfaction

Is there a one-size-fits-all approach to client satisfaction? By now you know the answer. You satisfy your clients one by one, moment by moment. As you know by now, you must step into your client's shoes and walk through your practice, seeing through your client's eyes and hearing with your client's ears.

You must adopt your client's perspective because what you may consider a satisfactory or successful outcome may not be how your client perceives it. You know what a serious impact it can have when you and your client don't see eye to eye. You know that clients' satisfaction affects how you and the care you've given them are evaluated and also clients' compliance and even the outcome. You know that your staff is important in this picture because clients judge you by your staff, and sometimes they'll stick with a veterinarian because of the staff.

Moving Forward

Quality management gives you a sense of moving forward, a structure and a process. It gives you confidence. Improving service quality isn't easy. It means change, and people don't accept change easily. The human brain becomes patterned to sameness, adapted to predictability. Change means work ("You want me to think new thoughts, move in new directions, create new paradigms? No thanks, I'll do it the old way.") Expect resistance, and prepare for it by melding individual values and goals with organizational values and goals. Quality service breeds pride, satisfaction, and success.

Now that you know all of this, you qualify as an expert—a Certified Client-Satisfying Veterinarian (that's a CCSV if you're into lots of letters after your name). Like other certifications, though, this one requires lots of continuing education credits. To maintain quality, you must keep moving, continually improving. So don't let your reading stop here.

You've taken the first step of the quality journey by reading this book. Our goal has been to give you an overview of customer satisfaction and quality service concepts as well as to introduce you to the techniques and tactics other veterinarians are using with success. We sincerely hope that you will consider investing in a one-way ticket—because once you begin the journey to quality service and success in your practice, you'll never want to turn back.

Notes

1. P. Pritchett. *Service Excellence!* Dallas: Pritchett & Associates, Inc., 1991.
2. P. Cohen, editor. Hard Work/Hard Play Makes Chiat/Day/Mojo a Dull Place — Not! *On Achieving Excellence*, 7(9) 1992: 2–4.
3. A. Ashby. Town and Country Veterinary Clinic. AAHA *Trends*, May 1994:11–12.